Planetary
Resonance

Everything Leaves a Trace

Dorothy Oja

Copyright © 2012 Dorothy Oja

All rights reserved. No part of this work may be reproduced, stored in a retrieval system, reprinted, or transmitted in any form or by any means electronic, mechanical, photocopying, scanning, recording, or otherwise without prior written permission from Dorothy Oja.
Reviewers may quote brief passages.

Requests for permission should be addressed to DOja07@gmail.com

Cover design by Eva Brunette
Cover Art by Dorothy Oja
Edited by Sheri Hartstein
Design, dtp and production by Loretta Lopez
Charts sourced by Solar Fire Software
Printed and bound in the United States of America

ISBN: 978-0-9790844-4-7

To the Future of Astrology

*"To believe in something not yet proved
and to underwrite it with our lives;
it is the only way
we can leave the future open."*

— Lillian Smith

Acknowledgements

Krista and Frank Woodward for making their beautiful Maui, Hawaii home available to finish the first draft of this book, and their excited support for the project. Georgia Stathis for early, middle and late encouragement and various and sundry important suggestions. John Flagg for editorial, spiritual, and fiscal support. Donna Van Toen, who trusted me enough to allow me to present the first rudimentary explanation of this method at SOTA, in Canada, so long ago. Monica Dimino, who grasped the concept right away and helped me out when I stumbled with my explanations that first time presenting Planetary Resonance. Bruce Scofield for asking probing, critical questions and encouraging me to change the name, which I did not do. (Sorry, Bruce!) The Power Book Sisters and my SIS (sisters in sanity): my remarkable six women-friends for watching me evolve over the 15 years of our group life to the culmination of this book. Thank you for witnessing and being supportive. Melanie Reinhart, who generously discussed bookmaking with me and gave me tips for publishing. Darby Costello, who supported my desire to write and heard my concept. Julene Packer, who believed in my ideas enough to ask me to teach them through the International Academy of Astrology (IAA). My super-smart students at IAA who willingly learned something brand new and rather alien ;*).

The wonderful women of the AstroDivas for their supportive words and energy sent across the miles and ethers. All my esteemed colleagues, whose books I've read throughout my astrological career that inspired my great desire to join them in authoring a book (my first but not my last!) Bernadette Brady and Darrelyn Gunzburg, who listened and encouraged my desire to complete this book. Lois Graessle, fellow writer, who knows and commiserated and supported the process. Those who came to my lectures on Planetary Resonance over the past years and were enthused and open to a new way of perceiving. Lisa Sanda for her quiet belief in me. Claire-France Perez for her generous spirit and endless ideas. Cathy Hand, who volunteered to help me with some essential last minute technical programming. Eva Atkins-Brunette for her unique visual and conceptual talent in helping me craft the vision for the book cover. My dear clients, who have taught me with their varied and rich life stories, and graced me with their trust. My three spectacular daughters: my ruby, Lisa, my emerald, Krista, and my blue diamond, Eva: you are my greatest achievement and my greatest life's gift. My favorite granddaughter, McKenna, who is well on the way to being a powerful writer; and my favorite grandson, Jake, who can be anything he wants to be.

To my mother Rose and grandmother Josepha – great Aquarian spirits and strong women, who were way ahead of their time and who taught me to believe and to endure.

My fabulous editor, Sheri Hartstein, and layout wizard, Loretta Lopez. Truly, this book would not have made it into print without your pragmatic and steady counsel and skill.

I hope I haven't left anyone out because I appreciated every bit of help received. Thank you to everyone from all my heart (not just the bottom)

TABLE OF CONTENTS

ix   Introduction

1   Everything Leaves a Trace - Everything Leaves a Residue 1

2   The Three Transformers Leave a Strong Background Residue 11

3   Continuum 17

4   Finding Your Birth Planetary Resonance 23

5   Post-Birth Planetary Resonance 31

6   Life Trajectory - Mapping the Resonant Influences 39

7   The Role of Saturn and Jupiter as Sub-cycles of Planetary Resonance 47

8   Using Planetary Resonance 55

9   Calculating Planetary Resonance 61

10   More Examples: Public Figures/Event 67

Introduction

A human being is part of the whole, called by us "universe," limited in time and space. He experiences himself, his thoughts and feelings as something separated from the rest – a kind of optical delusion of his consciousness. This delusion is a prison, restricting us to our personal desires and to affection for a few persons close to us. Our task must be to free ourselves from our prison by widening our circle of compassion to embrace all humanity and the whole of nature in its beauty.

—Albert Einstein

During my 2010 workshop on Planetary Resonance in San Francisco, someone asked me how I came to create this method. Since that time I've been trying to remember exactly how it all came about...

It was time to prepare a lecture for a conference and I wanted to present something new – something about Mars and identity – how identity is created and developed over a lifetime. As I was contemplating this, the importance and significant impact of the three outer planets registered in a different way than it had previously. I wanted to explore these contacts over the course of a lifetime to see how these might shape one's primary planet of identity – Mars. To the best of my recollection it all began with a series of musings. I questioned how personality energy is shaped, what shapes it, and when astrologically is the greatest impact. How exactly do we mature into who we are, and what would prompt powerful turning points? The answer appeared to be the transits of Uranus, Neptune and Pluto.

The question of resonance and lingering effects evolved from there. True synthesis requires time, testing, utilization and integration. Planetary Resonance Phases describe this process.

> *"Wolfgang Pauli, awarded the Nobel Prize, who as a prominent physicist could certainly not be accused of being a mystic visionary, stated in the year 1957: 'Contrary to the idea, propagated since the 17th Century, of the strict division of human thought into certain and separate categories, I should deem the striving to overcome the contradictions, and reaching the synthesis of rational comprehension and the mystic unity of experience, to be the explicit or unexplicit myth of our day and age.'"*
>
> — Theodor Landscheidt
> *Cosmic Cybernetics, The Foundations of a Modern Astrology*[1]

Neptune in Pisces, here at last, to blur the boundaries and remind us again that magic is alive in the universe, that all is not as it seems; that there is a vast and subtle, pulsing grid of energy always influencing us, even as it shimmers in the background.

Dorothy Oja, Boston, MA   May 2012

Note: The following abbreviations are used in all Planetary Resonance Case Study Examples.

t. = Transit
SR = Stationary Retrograde, SD = Stationary Direct
For Aspects: conj. = conjunction; sq. = square; opp = opposition
For House positions: House 7 becomes H7

---

[1] Dr. Theodor Landscheidt, *Cosmic Cybernetics, The Foundations of a Modern Astrology*; Ebertin-Verlag, 1973.

CHAPTER I

Everything Leaves a Trace — Everything Leaves a Residue

"A person should consider how things begin. A particular beginning results in a particular end."

—*The Bonesetter's Daughter* by Amy Tan

There's no such thing as living in a vacuum. We've advanced far beyond those ancient times of isolated existence, and even then the ancients knew that our environments impact, inform, sustain or destroy us.

It's common knowledge that we are affected by everything that surrounds us: not only our outer environment - personal and global, immediate and distant - but also our inner environment and the emotions of people close to our own auric/energetic field. Even those influences that are for the most part unseen have a powerful effect on the way we conduct our lives. These unseen energies are comprised of pure energy or sensation. We may not know exactly what to call them, how to categorize them, or why they work, but we have plenty of evidence of their existence and their effect. The influences of the planets are, of course, a prime example.

> *"The unanimous message of the mystics of all ages that all entities in the universe are interconnected and constitute an indivisible whole is proven now by unequivocal physical experiments that have been replicated again and again."*
>
> — Theodor Landscheidt
> *Sun-Earth-Man, A Mesh of Cosmic Oscillations*[1]

Einstein's Unified Field Theory ~ or "as above, so below"

I'm borrowing a term from Einstein and applying it to astrology. The idea of a unified field (wholeness) and that any one energy within a field affects every other energy in that field. This is nothing startling to anyone who has kept up with the new theories postulated by science in the last century or so – such as the fact that the observer influences the observed. Many of us take this understanding for granted as being self-evident, while others still attempt to separate what happens in the cosmos, above and around us, from what occurs on terra firma, our planet Earth.

Unified Field Theory

> The term was coined by Einstein, who attempted to unify the general theory of relativity with electromagnetism, hoping to recover an approximation for quantum theory. A 'theory of everything' is closely related to unified field theory, but differs by not requiring the basis of nature to be fields, and also attempts to explain all physical constants of nature. (from *Wikipedia*)

---

[1] Dr. Theodor Landscheidt, Sun, Earth, Man: A Mesh of Cosmic Oscillations. London: Urania Trust, 1989.

Later, in his theory of special relativity, Albert Einstein was able to explain the unity of electricity and magnetism as a consequence of the unification of space and time into an entity we now call spacetime.

(from *Wikipedia*)

We can extrapolate Einstein's theory by stating that everything that contacts us leaves a trace, a sample of itself, a piece of its own identity blended with ours. Consider special relationships or experiences you've had – haven't they left imprints on your life and psyche? Your emotions and your thinking? For better or worse, we are always pulsing with the combined influences of all that has touched us – body, mind, heart and spirit. This understanding informs the concept of *Planetary Resonance*, an idea that I've been developing for over 12 years.

Within the concept of Planetary Resonance are many other implications, once we delve into its patterns and chambers. There is room for further research and development of these ideas. But for now, there are two main dimensions of *Planetary Resonance* that I want to share with you and explain: **One concerns the present and how it influences the future. And the other is the past and how it has influenced the present.**

If we consider the wave nature of the universe, then everything affects everything else: all vibrations reverberate, bump into each other, continuously interacting and affecting everything ad infinitum. I offer *Planetary Resonance* as a small beginning toward that concept of a wave nature of astrology, and also the understanding of a ***continuum*** (which I will discuss further later in this book). Many scientists and great thinkers are studying the nature of the unified field as defined by Einstein, the wave theory and the study of cycles, and relating it to other disciplines. *Planetary Resonance* helps to map the residual influences of combining energies.

Defining Planetary Resonance

The essence of Planetary Resonance is two-fold. First, the three outermost planets – Uranus, Neptune and Pluto[1]– are the grand transformative triumvirate in modern astrology. In short, they govern awakening, transcendence, and metamorphosis, and have the greatest impact for change in the life of an individual, country, business entity, or even an animal, when they make dynamic aspects to the natal planets in the birth chart.

Second, *contacts from these three outer planets to any one of your five inner planets leave a distinct residual trace, and last for much longer than the actual mathematical ending of the transit.*

As astrologers, we are trained from the start to map the beginning of a powerful transit and then to determine exactly when it will end. However, my premise is that the transit influence lasts much longer than the numerical/mathematical value of its movement and exact contact with the natal planet.

The outer planet is the catalyst, beginning and inviting a change process. The resultant energy emitted from the contact and combination is its resonance.

One of the ways resonance is defined in the dictionary is as "a quality of evoking response." The transiting planet makes its mathematical contact and evokes a response from the contacted planet; their energies engage, then merge, and something new is created. The two energies must blend and cooperate in a new and different way, to reach a new understanding or a fresh perspective. At best, the inner planet seeks to understand the message of the outer planet and to adjust to the new alchemy.

---

[1] Although Pluto has been reassigned by a group of only 150 scientists to the status of dwarf planet, astrologers have been mapping its cycles since it was discovered in 1930 and have seen its impact in personal lives and world events. Scientists met to review their definition of "Planet" and Pluto's status change emerged from that. It was a controversial shift and the definition may yet be revised in the future.

As with all of life's engagements or relationships, the birth condition of the contacted planet affects the quality of the subsequent resonance produced.

Energy emits an essence, an essential part of itself. There are always residues. Something is always left behind. Forensic criminologists and CSI[2] viewers know this and so do astrologers! Once contact has been made, a relationship is forged and even though the relationship ends, residues are left behind – something is forever changed, transmuted and transformed.

Take the example of a house and the energies it holds from previous inhabitants and actions that may have taken place there. These residues linger and are often felt energetically or emotionally by the new residents and visitors to the house.

It is in part this knowledge that brought me to discover and formulate the method I've named *Planetary Resonance*. This *resonance* I define as the residual energy emitted and the traces left behind from powerful contacts between planets. *Powerful contacts* in this context refers to the Ptolomeic, or hard aspects of conjunction, square and opposition only (often referred to as the "fourth harmonic aspects").

Because of their intrinsic life-altering power, the transits of Uranus, Neptune and Pluto leave strong residual energy in their wake. Think of how a crystal glass resonates a tone when it is contacted, or the tones emitted from the reverberating strings of a guitar.

Once a resonance from a planetary contact is established, it can be mapped and cycles or life-phases are formed.

---

[2] CSI - Crime Scene Investigation is a breakthrough American crime drama television series. The show uses physical evidence to solve grisly murders in an unusually graphic way. In 2011, CSI was noted as the most watched drama series in the world.

Mapping Planetary Resonance Phases:

A planetary resonance from one of the outer three transformative planets lasts until the next contact from one of the three outermost planets to the same inner planet.

These cycles vary in length from months to many years, depending on where the three outer planets are located at any given time and the birth location of the inner planet being analyzed.

A contact is both a catalyst and a simultaneous blending of energies.

- A hard-aspect transit lasts until the next hard-aspect transit.

- The next conjunction, square, or opposition transit begins a new cycle of resonance with the birth planet.

- The **resonance** morphs once another hard aspect forms to the same planet.

Planetary Resonance **maps a planet's response cycle. We place a cyclic focus on one inner planet at a time.**

Example I: MARK ZUCKERBERG

As an example, we'll use the chart of Mark Zuckerberg, creator of Facebook, and examine his birth Mars position. His birth Mars is at 19° Scorpio. Facebook was launched on 2/4/04, when Zuckerberg was nearly 20 years old.

The first transiting aspect from either Uranus, Neptune or Pluto to Zuckerberg's Mars at 19° Scorpio was a conjunction from Pluto on 12/14/90. (We'll discuss the *Mars Resonance he came in with at birth* in a later chapter.) This conjunction of Pluto to his Mars

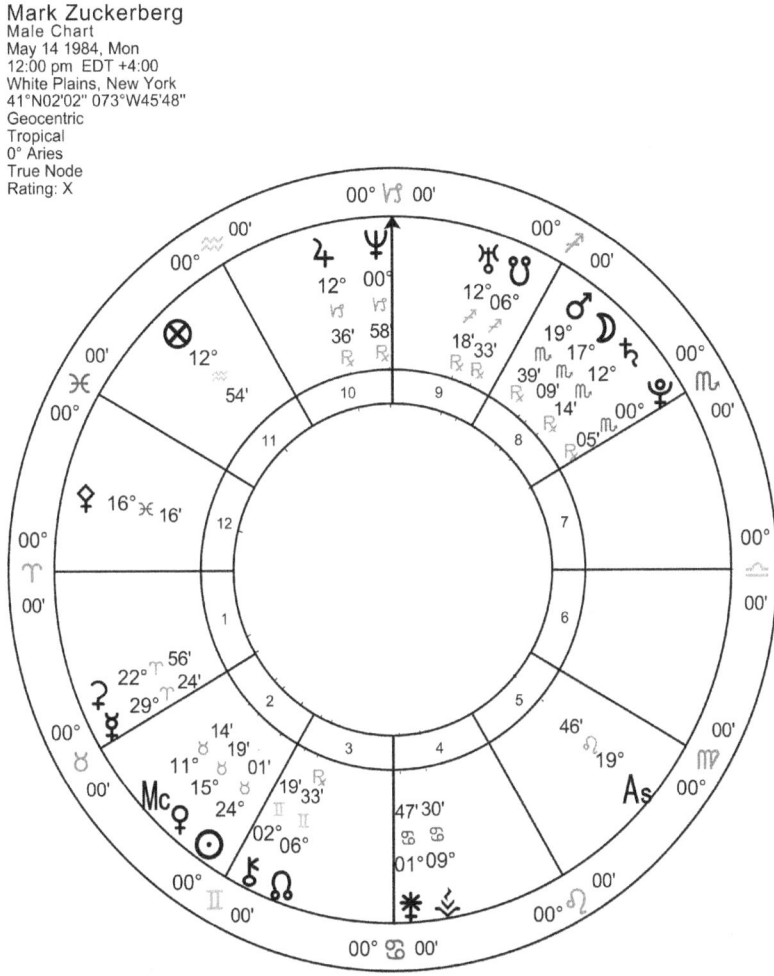

occurred at age 6. The *Pluto Resonance Phase* lasted until 3/28/06 (age nearly 22), when transiting Neptune/Aquarius squared his Mars/Scorpio and this became the next *Mars Resonance Phase*. Facebook was founded during Zuckerberg's *Pluto Resonance Phase*.

Choosing to use Mars as the example planet for Zuckerberg is intended to show the development of his identity, impetus, and thrust into life. Having a *Pluto Resonance* so early in life stimulated his focus and the development of his resources. By all accounts he was a nerdy, brilliant kid able to train his energies to research deeply whatever interested him. His father taught him Atari basic programming and then hired a software developer to tutor him. (The tutor called him a prodigy and said it was hard to stay ahead of him.) Zuckerberg also studied the classics and is fluent in numerous languages.

Once transiting Pluto made that conjunction to Zuckerberg's Mars, the two planetary energies merged and worked together in the background of his life – reverberating, evolving, and developing him in a Plutonian frequency for 15+ years – until a *Neptune Resonance* replaced it and a distinct change in direction (Mars) was mandated.

Example II: BARACK OBAMA

We'll be examining Obama's Venus at 1º Cancer.

Barack Obama was born on 8/4/61 at 7:24 PM, Honolulu, HI (RR: AA from Birth Certificate)

Shortly before his historic election as the new President of the United States in November of 2008, Obama's grandmother died. Astrologically, this was symbolized in part by transiting Pluto making an opposition aspect (180 degree angle) to his birth Venus in Cancer. The major influence of his grandmother left a void which was filled with the huge demands of the Presidency. This transit also suggests that he would have to transform his understanding of values (Venus), and describes the unique demands and challenges to his core values that the office of the Presidency would require of him. According to the principles of *Planetary Resonance*, Obama was entering a new *Pluto Resonance Phase to his birth Venus*. Obama's Pluto/Venus Resonance cycle lasted until Uranus/Aries squared his Venus at 1º Cancer in January 2012.

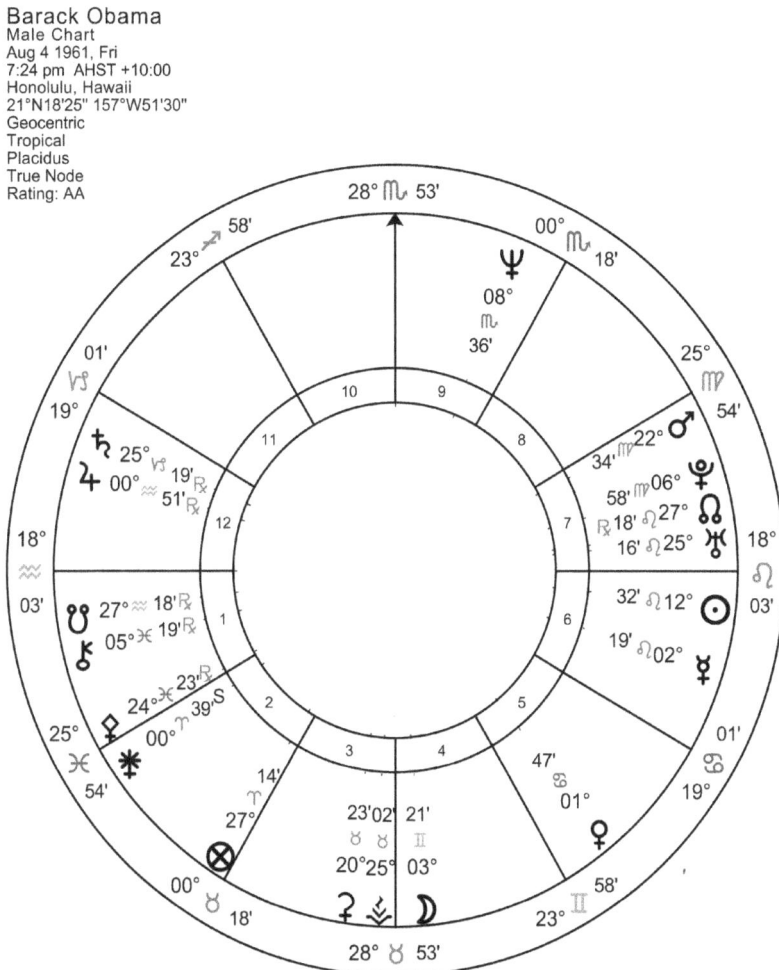

How is it relevant?

By beginning to think in terms of the more subtle influences of life – the resonances activated and their lingering effects – we are fulfilling some of the messages inherent in the transit of Neptune through Pisces, which invites a new consciousness of subtlety and nuance.

10 PLANETARY RESONANCE

CHAPTER 2

The Three Transformers Leave a Strong Background Residue

We are all fated to have Plutonian, Neptunian and Uranian experiences while we do our time on planet Earth. Contacts from these three outermost planets will represent the most profound times of our lives, dramatically transforming and shaping us, presenting us with complexities to challenge our sense of self, our innermost soul, and our role in the world. They affect all important events – social, economic, cultural and political – personal or collective.

Planetary Resonance considers the outermost planets to be the "wild cards" of the zodiac. They offer the most dramatic transformations of life. After years of astrological study, I am leaning more and more toward considering this triumvirate as separate entities, not necessarily rulers of any one sign. These three energetic transmissions are deeply significant of major transitions – cosmic invitations if you will – to reach higher levels of consciousness about self, soul and the environments we inhabit.

The foundation of *Planetary Resonance* **involves the movements and aspects of Uranus, Neptune and Pluto in relation to your five inner or personality planets: Sun, Moon, Mercury, Venus or Mars.** *Planetary Resonance* begins when one of the transiting outer planets contacts one of your inner planets by **conjunction, square or**

opposition only (the hard aspects or Ptolemaic aspects).[1] All calculations with this method are based on the exact degree of your natal inner five planets.

Each of the three outer planets season each of the five inner planets to impart intrinsic life lessons – leading (potentially) to wisdom, compassion and understanding of the complexities and nuances of life's various adventures and mishaps. At that moment of contact by transit, a resonance relationship is established. That specific resonance is either Uranian, Neptunian or Plutonian in nature, and its energy remains active until the next transiting aspect of an outer planet contacts that same inner planet.

Qualities

If we're analyzing an inner planet in Barack Obama's chart, for example, for applying *Planetary Resonance*, then we need to determine when either Uranus, Neptune, or Pluto are in a cardinal sign, as planets in cardinal signs will deliver the hard aspects (or 4th harmonic angle) we are using. This will then begin a new resonance cycle for that planet – in our example, Venus/Cancer. The same logic applies to planets in fixed or mutable signs.

Let's examine Barack Obama's birth Venus at 1º Cancer for its most recent *Planetary Resonance Phases*.

According to the principles of Planetary Resonance, Barack Obama entered a new Pluto Resonance Phase to his birth Venus on 12/25/08. Obama's Pluto/Venus Resonance cycle lasted until transiting Uranus/Aries squared his Venus at 1º Cancer in January 2012.

---

[1] Major mathematical aspects between planets as defined by astrologer/mathematician Claudius Ptolemy (c. AD 90 - c. AD 168).

The Three Transformers Leave a Strong Background Residue 13

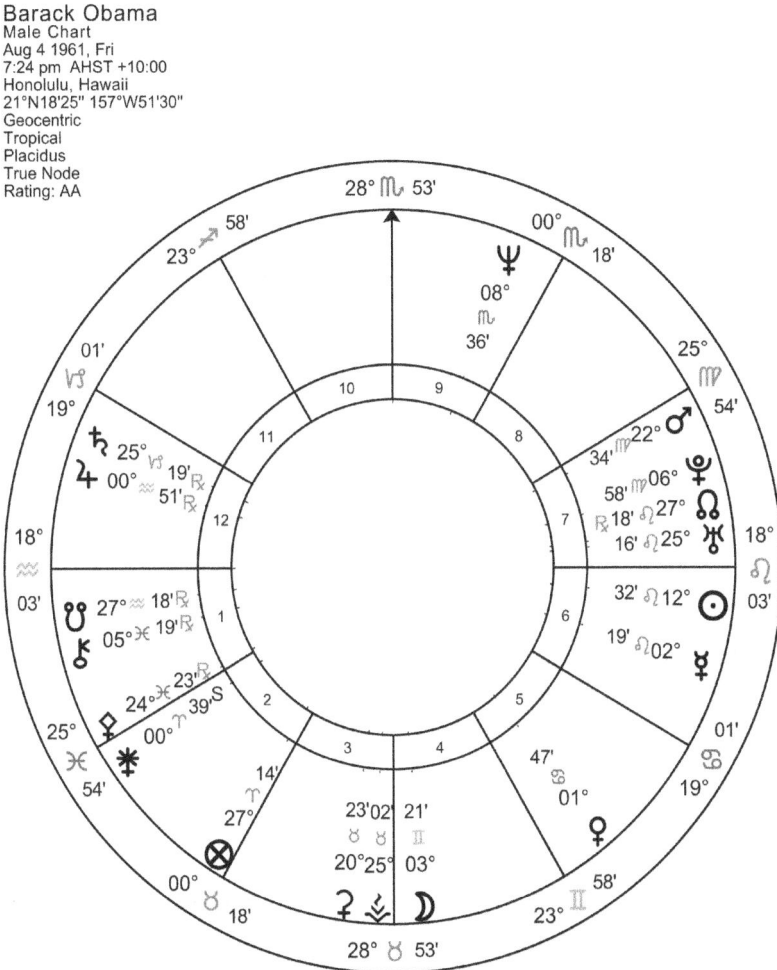

Shortly after Obama's historic election as President of the United States (11/4/08), transiting Pluto/Capricorn made its first opposition to his Venus on 12/25/08, initiating a new phase of *Planetary Resonance* in relation to his Venus. Because it was a Pluto Resonance Phase, this required Obama to transform his relationships and his values on a very deep level. His maternal grandmother's death just days before he was elected was surely part of this transformative cycle, symbolized in part by transiting Pluto making an opposition aspect (180 degree angle) to his birth Venus in Cancer. The effect of transiting Pluto would be to transform his understanding of values and his relational skills (Venus), and the opposition implies his instilled sense of principles and diplomacy would be intensely challenged especially through his dealings with 11th house organizations and groups and the entire issue of values as it applies to financial deficit.

If we look at the deeper meaning, we might say that Obama was now required to fully incorporate the legacy of love and relationship values that he received from his maternal grandmother, his mother, his wife, and indeed from all the influential women in his past. Much of Pluto's transmissions are unconscious unless one is willing to delve deeper and probe its promptings. All of Obama's relationships from that time forward would be undergoing a deep Plutonic purging and metamorphosis. The new demands of presidential political relationships were thrust upon him and he had to change and adjust his sense of how to relate, which was certainly quite different from what he might have anticipated. Indeed, his struggles for cooperation and compromise within Congress made news on a regular basis.

Pluto/Capricorn replaced Obama's prior *Uranus Resonance Phase* with Venus, which had been active since Uranus/Capricorn opposed his Venus in early December 1988 – a period of 20 years. This exemplifies how some *Planetary Resonance Phases* endure for a long time. As it turns out, based on the movements of the outer planets, Obama's *Pluto Resonance Phase* to his Venus would be a short one, lasting just over two years.

In 2011, transiting Uranus/Aries made a waning square to Obama's Venus/Cancer and began yet another *Planetary Resonance* to his Venus (another Uranus cycle!) This *Uranus Resonance* Phase will last until April 2025, when it will be replaced by transiting Neptune/Aries.

As this Obama example shows, because of the slow movement of the three outer planets, subsequent contacts initiating new Planetary Resonance Phases can be years away, or sometimes only months or a short year or two, depending on how fast the outer planets are traveling at any given time. *I fondly call this the Western equivalent of Vedic planetary periods.* (Being a Western humanistic astrologer, I've always been a bit envious of the Vedic Planetary Periods and knew that there had to be a Western Astrology counterpart or equivalent!)

No matter what else is happening, the inner planet is still resonating with and processing the energy transmission of the last outer planet hard aspect contact. It's still on that vibrational resonance, operating subtly in the background, and it colors and conditions everything else (other types of transits) that contact that planet afterwards. The effect can be prolonged, as explained, and echoes through the psyche until replaced by the next major hard aspect transit from another one of the three outer planets.

One of the many benefits of this system is that *it can be used effectively even without an accurate birthtime!* There is much that you can learn about the core dynamics of a person's life focus and lessons, desires and needs, by applying this system to the position of their Sun, Mercury, Venus and Mars. The Moon, however, because of its potential 12-13 degree movement per day, will be more elusive and less accurate when applying *Planetary Resonance*, unless you have an exact or near exact birth time.

"When information is received, and this is inevitable when one entity enters the transmitting range of another differentiated entity, a reciprocal effect comes about: A wandering electron, for example, approaches a proton and together they form a hydrogen atom. The male approaches the female and together they make up a more complex structure, and so forth. In none of these forms of reciprocation, be they primitive or highly complex, do the three essential aspects of the existential substance – the material, the energetic, the structural, the informational – become separate from one another, although man has often attempted to do just this for misunderstood reasons of simplification.

The American researcher Robert B. Evans *expressly points out that information and energy are inseparably connected. There are no information processes without the expenditure of energy, and there is no transformation of energy without information. Matter is also included in this coherence through the* Einstein formula $E = MC2$. *With it, too, the material function and the informational processes are indivisible…"*

— Theodor Landscheidt, *Cosmic Cybernetics*

CHAPTER 3

Continuum

*"We shall not cease from exploration
And the end of all our exploring
Will be to arrive where we started
And know the place for the first time."*

—T.S. Eliot, *Four Quartets*

By applying the technique of Planetary Resonance, we can easily move toward the concept of continuum: thinking of the chart as a continuum, a continuation. There is no such thing as an abrupt stop or start – all moments in time are part of a continuation of something that came before, and a movement toward something that is yet to come.

As astrologers we are used to looking at the birth chart of an individual as the beginning of a life, and in one sense that is completely true. And yet, in another sense, it is merely a continuation of time past. It is a moment that is captured, frozen in time like a photograph; but time never stops – it has a past and it has a future- and both past and possibility are contained in the birth moment and within each planetary degree. This is the nature of a continuum.

> *"What we call the beginning is often the end*
> *And to make an end is to make a beginning."*
>
> — T.S.Eliot, *Four Quartets*

Every degree in your birth chart exists on a continuum. Each degree resonates with what has come before and what will come next, and at each moment we are attuning to both the past and the present – we weave back and forth, forward and backward, integrating the sensations of past and future. The idea of a continuum of planetary degrees in the birth chart is further illustrated when we examine the Planetary Resonance each of your inner planets holds and carries from the past into the birth moment.

An example from a recent event in the news illustrates this point: The tragic death of Trayvon Martin, a 17-year-old boy shot by George Zimmerman, a neighborhood watch captain, on 2/26/12 in Sanford, Florida. (Trayvon Martin was born on 2/5/95 in Miami, FL, time unknown. George Zimmerman was born on 10/5/83 in Manassas, VA, time unknown.)

Zimmerman is a Libra with Mercury at 24º Virgo and Mars at 3º Virgo – the exact degree at which Mars was set to turn direct on 4/13/12. This is an example of how one can be responsive and sensitive to planetary degree points (especially station points) before the actual station takes place. This condition in Zimmerman's chart placed greater focus on his actions, or his willingness to act, or perhaps his impulsiveness (Mars). Transiting Mercury was at 23º Pisces, the degree at which it would also later turn direct, giving credence to the "shadow" or foreshadowing cycle of planets, and also sensitizing the potential confusion and misinterpretation (Pisces) of the meeting between the two victims in this tragic story.

This example illustrates that a planet responds to its next (future) station point! Logic would tell us that planets also respond to past triggers.

☐←←←←←←←22 Virgo→→→→→→→☐

Barack Obama's Mars is at 22° Virgo. During the triple retrogrades of Mars/Virgo, Mercury/ Pisces and Venus/Gemini in the first half of 2012 – all of which had station points at 23 degrees of mutable signs (within one degree of Obama's birth Mars position), President Obama's signature legislation – the Patient Protection and Affordable Care Act – went to the Supreme Court to be challenged for constitutionality. Other than the re-election campaign itself, all this focus on Obama's Mars would clearly bring attention to his initiatives, actions and goals. Once we accept that time is a continuum, it is easier to understand how the past still influences the patterns in the birth chart. In other words, the past is contained and maintained as an imprint therein. Planetary Resonance shows how this works.

It's the same for the future. We are influenced and magnetized by the pull of both the past and the future. We are pulled backwards and forwards all the time, responding to both ends of the continuum spectrum.

All the major events keyed in by planetary stations around 23° of mutable signs - personal and collective - are linked to the time when Neptune in Pisces reaches that degree in May 2021.

> *"Time present and time past*
> *Are both perhaps present in time future,*
> *And time future contained in time past."*
>
> — T.S. Eliot, *Four Quartets*

Definition of Continuum

A coherent whole characterized as a collection, sequence, or progression of values or elements varying by minute degrees "good" and "bad"...stand at opposite ends of a continuum instead of describing the two halves of a line. (*Merriam Webster Dictionary*)

Time - the continuum of experience in which events pass from the future through the present to the past

History - the continuum of events occurring in succession leading from the past to the present and even into the future; "all of human history." (*The Free Dictionary by Farlex*)

Resonance with Significant Historical Events via Planetary Stations

The easiest way to reference your connection with past historical events or time periods is to look back in the ephemeris for planetary stations made by Uranus, Neptune or Pluto, and determine whether any of those stations made a strong contact to one of the planets in your chart. (Use exact contacts to start, see what you find, and then go to stations that are within a one degree orb.) You can do this for any planet, as they all make station points (except for the luminaries). However, I suggest you begin with stations of the three outer planets and see if they match up by conjunction, square or opposition with any of your natal planets. That correlation point will represent a potential past resonance that may trigger your interest in that time period in history and exert a subconscious influence on your awareness and personality in the present.

For instance, I was born with Venus at 25° Cancer and when searching backward in time, I found that Pluto/Cancer made a station exactly at 25° Cancer in April of 1936. A chill ran through me because I had always had an intense fascination with WWII and felt I had a prior life during that time as part of the French or Dutch resistance movement. Of course I cannot prove that I actually lived back then, but the astrological correlation provides a compelling resonance factor. Very often we intuitively feel this resonance from the past without any logical reason. *Planetary Resonance* offers a possible explanation for this attraction towards particular historical periods.

In addition, looking backwards in time prior to your birth to explore significant outer planet transits to your birth chart provides insight into the Planetary Resonance you were born pulsating with – for each one of your personal planets! This will be explained further in another chapter.

> "[There is a] metaphorical resonance to significant historical events."
>
> (from *Latitudes* Magazine, March/April 2011)

Once we accept that time is a continuum, it is easier to understand how the past still influences the patterns in the birth chart. In other words, the past is contained - still exists - just as the future is a possibility.

> *"The role which the number plays in mythology and in the unconscious provides food for thought. It is one aspect of the physically real as well as of the psychic imagination. It is not only a unit of counting or measuring, it is not merely quantitative in character, it is also a qualitative expression and is therefore a mysterious cross between myth and reality, on the one hand discovered and on the other invented."*
>
> — Carl Gustav Jung[1]

---

[1] *C. G. Jung, "Civilization in Transition," Collected Works (Vol. 10) (Princeton, NJ: Bollingen, 1934)*

One of my objectives in writing *Planetary Resonance* is to open doors and windows to the merging of both myth and reality. We can stay in the pure realm of numbers, or we can interpret these same numbers as symbols of resonances that operate in the background of our lives, exerting a subtler, yet profound effect. Magic, the soul, synchronicity, and even the seemingly inexplicable mysteries of existence are the historical foundation of astrology, as well as the way we can continue our astrological journey into the future. *Planetary Resonance* is one way to explore that option.

CHAPTER 4

Finding Your Birth Planetary Resonance

Your Birth Planetary Resonance is Found Before You Were Born

Planetary Resonance presumes that you enter life not with a blank slate, but with a specific resonance attached to each one of your personal planets. Essentially, each of us is resonating with a prior contact made to the exact degree of our personal natal planets at the moment we are born. This resonance can be mapped and calculated and results in identifying your *Birth Planetary Resonance*.

How to Find your Birth Planetary Resonance

Look back in your ephemeris to the time before you were born when one of the three outer planets – Uranus, Neptune or Pluto – made the last contact to one of your inner planets. Search for the prior major aspect (conjunction, square or opposition) *closest* to your birthdate to either your natal Sun, Moon, Mercury, Venus or Mars. *(If you have Solar Fire, you can use the Animate Chart function to go backward and forward. Another computer calculation function will be explained later).* Even though as astrologers we are most familiar discussing the future via upcoming transits, any planetary degree in the natal chart is still sensitive to a past influence, just as it is sensitive to a future influence.

Along the continuum we explained previously, we are using the closest exact aspect to the central point, which is the planetary degree we are exploring. From the past we use the *last* time the aspect was exact, and for the future we use the *first* exact contact by aspect.

x(last)------------------Mars 22° Virgo-----------------(first)x

Obama's Birth Mars at 22° Virgo – House 7

We'll use Barack Obama's 22° Mars/Virgo as our example to illustrate this concept. For the *Birth Planetary Resonance* in Obama's chart, we are looking for the last transit to 22° Virgo from either Uranus, Neptune or Pluto *before* his actual birth. In the case of a retrograde planet, we will use the closest (the last) exact contact to 22° Virgo *before* birth.

The last transit of an outer planet to Obama's natal Mars degree, prior to his birth, was Uranus at 22° Gemini in April, 1948. So, Uranus is Barack Obama's *Birth Resonance* to his natal Mars.

We place this past Uranus at 22° Gemini in his birth chart and analyze its condition. Its position created a waxing square from his House 4 to his House 7 Mars.

An interpretation of this contact is easily seen in view of what we know of Obama's biography. Since we are using the inner planet Mars, which is responsible for the development of identity (among other things), we can interpolate as follows: Obama was destined to experience disruption around the martial or "masculine" identity factor in his personality. The position of Uranus in House 4 suggests the home/family environment as the source of this disruption. We know that his parents were a mixed race couple and divorced when Obama was around the age of one. He only saw his birth father once

Finding Your Birth Planetary Resonance 25

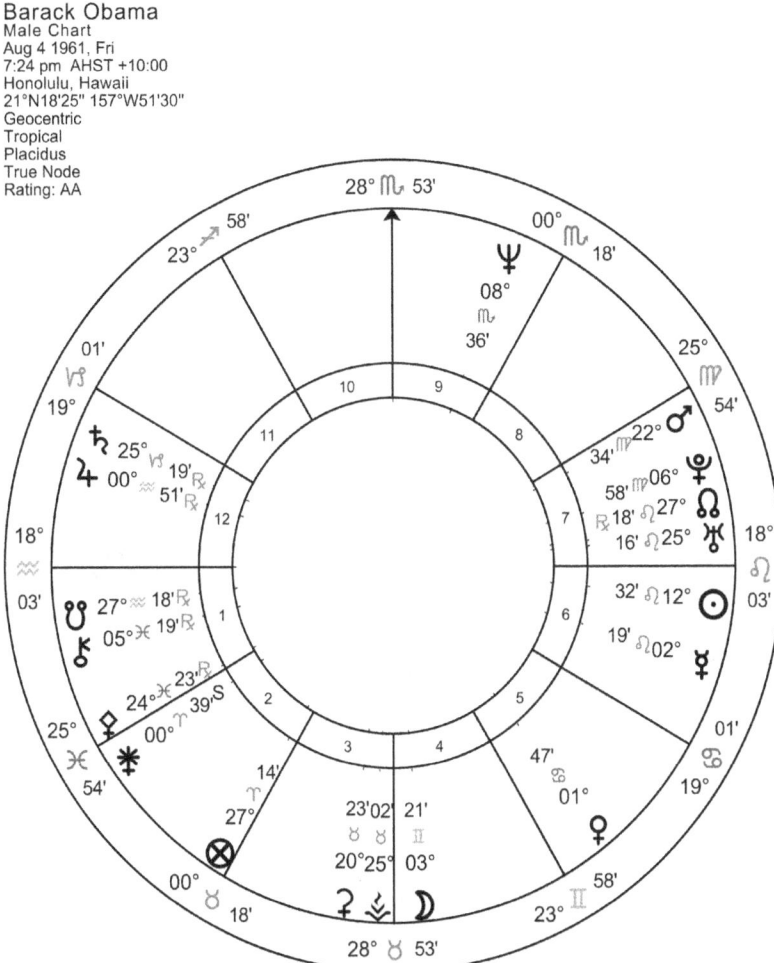

after that in 1971. His mother remarried and the family moved to Indonesia, which surely represented a huge cultural disruption – but very likely also offered insights that could be applied later in life. He had a step-father and a half-sister. His mother's other relationships and her devotion to her work abroad led to Obama's eventual separation from her when he returned to live with his grandparents in the U.S. Then his mother died young, age 52, of uterine cancer. These are all possible scenarios with a pre-birth Uranus planetary resonance occurring in his House 4 in Gemini square his House 7 Mars/Virgo: family disruptions, separations and mixed messages about his identity and how to fit in, as well as the wound of an absent father.

Remember you have to combine the interpretation of the *Birth Resonance* with the planet it is being applied to. If we continue to use the example of Obama's Mars with a Uranus *Birth Resonance*, we can interpret this as a developmental challenge to integrate being different and valuing differences and moving to broad-mindedness and expressions of larger truth. The experience of loneliness or alienation would also be part of that challenge, as Uranus has to find its own beat in the song of life.

Obama's Uranus Birth Planetary Resonance to Mars lasted until he was 5 years and 2 months old. On 10/25/66, Uranus/Virgo made a conjunction to Obama's Mars at 22° Virgo. Thus, the first *Planetary Resonance* after his birth was also Uranian, but in a different configuration. This House 7 conjunction suggests an encounter or event that would have created an immediate jolt of awakening or awareness. It was at this time that the family moved to Indonesia and tapped into the promise of the *Uranus Birth Planetary Resonance:* multicultural experiences, shocks and disruptions that would shape his identity and potentially broaden his perspective and awareness.

The *Birth Resonance* is the core energy that part of the personality must master and experience. When the *Birth Resonance* repeats after birth it stimulates that core energy, highlighting those time periods as important phases in the development of the qualities represented by that planet. It is also a familiar time, reinforcing similar themes, because it is the resonance one came in with. One might feel more familiar energy and act accordingly, perhaps more boldly during one's *Birth Planetary Resonance* cycle in the ways shown by the resonance and its position and aspects in the natal chart.

Some Keyword Meanings for each *Birth Resonance*:

<u>Uranus Birth Resonance</u> – Separation can lead to perspective or aloofness. Shock can lead to awakening. Anti-Tribal/Counter-Culture can lead to originality/authenticity. Surprises and the unexpected can become the urge to individuate or invent, or fear of closeness. Uranus has a particular mission regarding truth and authenticity: to being one's own person but avoiding the complete loner syndrome, honoring the humanity in all beings; to being inclusive and having a broader perspective and a more objective viewpoint.

<u>Neptune Birth Resonance</u> – Heightened sensitivity can lead to compassion and understanding of subtleties others miss. Isolation/Aloneness can lead to spiritual development, faith or transcendence, or alcoholism, drugs, other negative escapes. Idealism can lead to the visionary and inspiring. Neglect, abuse or avoidance can lead to a relationship with the divinity in all, spiritual pursuits, or helping others overcome. Neptune has a particular mission to inspire, find meaning and unify, to serve or suffer.

<u>Pluto Birth Resonance</u> – Loss can lead to deepening the soul and surrendering to forces beyond one's control, and purging what we no longer need. Crises and profound emotional experiences can lead to empowerment, embracing vulnerability, transformation and resourcefulness. Powerlessness can lead to internal development, understanding power and control and its implications, or the desire to control and manipulate others. Obsession can lead to an understanding of our desires and motives. Pluto has a particular mission to use power and resources for good via strategy, research and developmental growth to have an impact, or leave a legacy.

Unfoldment and Assimilation

These lifetime *Planetary Resonance* phases identify both an unfoldment and an assimilation of energy that is transmitted by the three most powerful planetary energies when they make dynamic angles to your inner (personality) planets. This is a more subtle way to understand the effects of planets. Once ignited, my premise is that we hold these powerful energies and work with them - at the beginning, in a very obvious way when the aspect is fresh, but later in subtler ways that operate in the background like a quiet humming. We are learning the message of a Uranian, Neptunian or Plutonian transmission and it affects our responses, even though this may be unconscious or below awareness. This method sheds light on this subtler dynamic and provides answers to developmental cycles that may have been previously elusive. Some of the lessons, inspirations or dynamic transformations catalyzed by transits of Uranus, Neptune or Pluto take a long time (years), as indicated by the varying length of time for these resonance phases to transfer from one to another. However, at other times the cycles can be much shorter in length, when two or all three of the outer planets are in the same modality: cardinal, fixed or mutable.

Uranus is the most common birth resonance, since it has the shortest cycle of the three, spending approximately 7 years in each sign, so you are likely to experience more Uranian Resonance Phases. What does it mean that Uranus is the most common birth resonance?... The energy of Uranus keeps us alert to being human by offering shocks and surprises to wake us up to the fact that we are here, living life on planet Earth. It is a creative force that focuses on uniqueness and individuality, and is a major catalyst of change.

We are likely to experience all three Planetary Resonances in our lifetime to any one of our five inner or personality planets.

Is one of your inner planets the oddity: the only one of the five resonating with a different outer planet *Birth Resonance*? What could this mean? Or is one outer planet missing as a birth resonance to one of your inner planets? What could this mean?

One of the things we learn early on in our study of astrology is that everything in the chart has significance. If one out of five of your inner planets is the only one resonating with a different outer planet energy (this is likely to be rare), we'd want to pay attention to that, take note, and realize that this inner planet is on a different learning track, while your other inner planets are humming the same basic tune.

When one of the three outer planet energies is missing as a *Birth Resonance* (this is a more typical occurrence), when it does occur later in the course of the life, it is more likely a new wave of understanding and energy transmission, and could be very surprising or complex for the person to assimilate in relation to the inner planet in question. As is the case with a missing element in astrology, the person may not need that element as much as the others to fulfill their destiny. So, it is the same with a missing *Birth Resonance*. However, there is another piece to this puzzle – the missing energy (much like a missing element or modality) will also provide challenges. When there is a *Resonance Phase* later in life of the missing *Birth Resonance*, it will be negotiated in a fresh and new way because it has not been previously instilled.

Planetary Resonance is a subtler form of working with planetary energy and it will take time getting used to implementing the technique, but I feel certain you will find value in it. In this chapter we've explained how to find your *Birth Resonance* from the three outer planets to any one of your five inner or personality planets. In the next chapter we will examine the post-birth *Resonance Phases*.

CHAPTER 5

Post-Birth Planetary Resonance

Now that we've found your *Birth Planetary Resonance*, it's time to discover and map the Resonance Phases that take place after your birthday and throughout your lifetime.

Planetary Resonance Phases after one's birth are calculated the same way as the **Birth Planetary Resonance**, except that we are now going forward in the ephemeris/computer and looking for the very first time there's an exact aspect from Uranus, Neptune or Pluto to the inner planet we are researching.

As before, we are looking for a conjunction, square or opposition only (Ptolomeic or 4th harmonic aspects) to one of the five inner "personality" planets (Sun, Moon, Mercury, Venus or Mars) that you've chosen to explore.

The first *Planetary Resonance* cycle after one's birth could be the same as the *Birth Planetary Resonance* cycle, or not – it all depends on the degree of the planet you are exploring and the signs and degrees that Uranus, Neptune and Pluto are traveling through at any given time.

Our Example from Chapter 4: The Chart of Barack Obama

It is interesting (but not all that unusual) to note that Obama's first *Planetary Resonance* to Mars after his birth does happen to be the same as his *Birth Resonance*. The Uranian energy transmission to Mars, his identity/initiative, is therefore accentuated and emphasized early in his developmental cycle.

Obama's Mars Birth Resonance: Uranus
(Uranus/Gemini sq. Mars 6/24/47 – duration 5 yrs. 2 mo.)

1. t.Uranus/Virgo conj. Mars/Virgo (H7)
10/25/66 at age 5 yrs. 2 mo. (duration 1 yr. 2.5 mo.)

Birth Resonance repeat.

Moved to Indonesia with mother and stepfather.

2. t.Pluto/Virgo conj. Mars/Virgo (H7)
11/23/67 at age 6 yrs. 2.5 mo. (duration 13 yrs.)

Sister Maya was born, moved back to Hawaii to live with grandparents, met birth father for first and only time, moved to L.A.

3. t.Neptune/Sag. sq. Mars/Virgo (H10)
3/5/80 at age 19 yrs. 6 mo. (duration 6+ yrs.)

Transferred to Columbia University in NYC, father died in car accident, graduated from Columbia.

4. t.Uranus/Sag. sq. Mars/Virgo (H10)
12/14/86 at age 25 yrs. 6 mo. (duration 18 yrs.)

Birth Resonance repeat.

First trip to Europe/Kenya. Entered Harvard Law School. Book published. Elected to IL Senate. Elected to US Senate. Married Michelle. Mother died. Two daughters born.

5. t.Pluto/Sag. sq. Mars/Virgo (H10)
12/27/04 at age 43 yrs. 4 mo. (duration 3.5 yrs.)

Returned to Kenya (second time). Announced his candidacy for President.

6. t.Uranus/Pisces opp. Mars/Virgo (H1)
6/12/08 at age 46 yrs. 9 mo. (duration 12 yrs.11 mo.)

Birth Resonance repeat.

Elected President of USA. Won the Nobel Prize for Peace.

7. t.Neptune/Pisces opp. Mars/Virgo (H1)
5/7/21 at age 59 yrs. 8 mo.

Planetary Resonance cycles last for varying lengths of time, always dependent on two factors: where planets are located currently in the cosmic schema, and the sign and degree of the planet being analyzed in your own birth chart. It is the duration of these planetary phases that allows for the development or evolution of these powerful transmissions of energy from Uranus, Neptune and Pluto.

Example: Steve Jobs. His Mars/Aries in House 8 (H8)

In analyzing the chart of Steve Jobs, I encountered a mathematical dilemma for my technique. Normally, I would only consider a *Resonance Phase* to begin at the exact mathematical number – in this case, Jobs' Mars at 29° Aries. However, when I looked back to locate the last outer planet that triggered that degree, I found that Neptune made a Station Retrograde at 28° which is less than a degree of an exact opposition to Jobs' Mars at 29°. Technically, Neptune never made it to the exact numerical degree 29 (until after his birth). This was a dilemma, and one could argue for the sake of consistency

34 PLANETARY RESONANCE

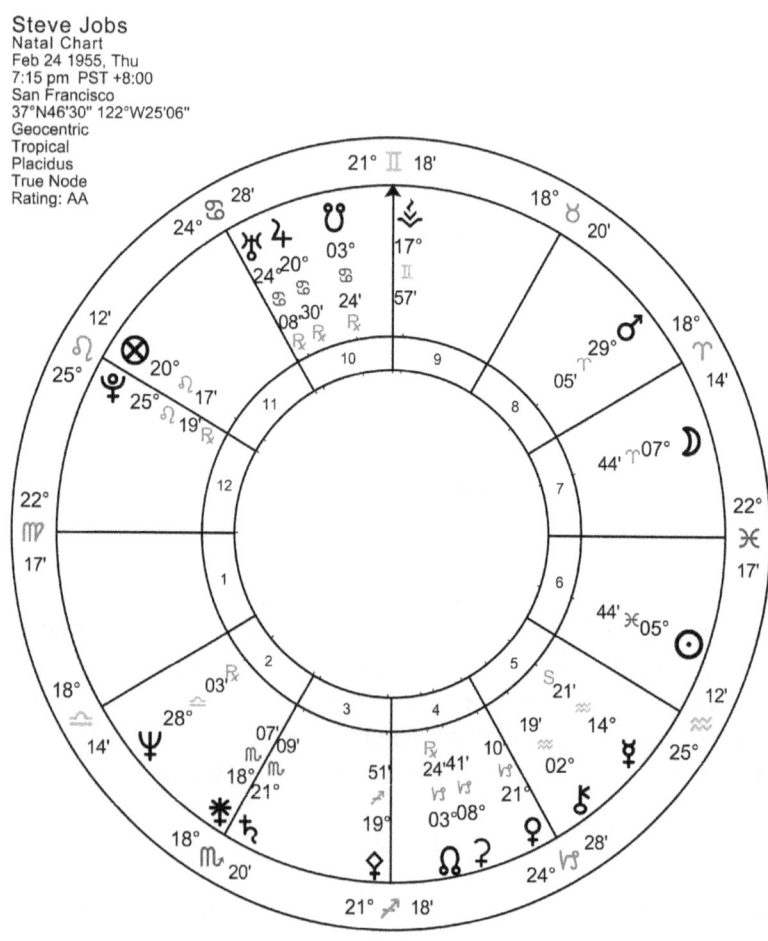

to search farther back in time to when Pluto/Cancer made an exact numerical aspect: a waxing square prior to his birth on 6/13/39. Still, there's room to consider Neptune as well.

Each number resonates, vibrates at a different level of energy.

> *"The number...belongs to two worlds, the real and the imaginary one; it is clear and it is obscure, it is quantitative and qualitative..."*
>
> — Carl Jacobi (German mathematician)

In Walter Isaacson's biography of Steve Jobs, he states: "I think his desire for complete control of whatever he makes derives directly from his personality and the fact that he was abandoned at birth," said longtime colleague, Del Yocam. "He wants to control his environment, and he sees the product as an extension of himself." In another quote from the book, Andy Hertzfeld, a friend of Jobs since the early 1980's said: "The key question about Steve is why he can't control himself at times from being so reflexively cruel and harmful to some people....That goes back to being abandoned at birth. The real underlying problem was the theme of abandonment in Steve's life."

These quotes sound much more like a **Pluto Birth Resonance** to Mars, as Pluto has a great deal to do with attachment, bonding, possessing, loss and abandonment. So, let's take a deeper look.

Steve Jobs' exact **Birth Resonance** to Mars was Pluto/Cancer (6/13/39) granting him a fierceness and unyielding determination to explore deeply whatever grabbed his interest. A Mars/Pluto Resonance is an intense investment of energy. If we look further at his chart, we see that this message is supported in several other ways, creating one of his central themes. Mars located in House 8 and trine to Pluto/Leo reinforces the Pluto Resonance to Mars. There is an underlying impulse in the personality to make a big difference. We can also add the position of Saturn/Scorpio – a legacy, debt or wound to overcome. Repressed anger and even cruelty can arise from the depths of Pluto-associated conditions, which the above quotes explicitly express.

Planetary Resonance Placements in the Chart

Subsequent Planetary Resonance cycles for Steve Jobs will most likely all take place in succedent houses (2, 5, 8, 11) because we are using only 4th harmonic aspect patterns.

Succedent Houses: These placements concern security, stability, investment of resources, and values by which one lives one's life.

Since Jobs' Mars/Aries is located in a cardinal sign, the 4th harmonic transiting aspects from Uranus, Neptune or Pluto must also be in cardinal signs to make the next *Planetary Resonance Phase* aspect.

Angular Houses (1, 4, 7, 10): These are the houses that are the most active and the most visible, projecting people into the limelight and action.

Cadent Houses (3, 6, 9, 12): These houses revolve around ideas, learning, beliefs and belief systems, and gathering and disseminating information through speech, communication of any kind, and all forms of media.

A brief interpretation for Steve Jobs' natal Mars position would go something like this: A cardinal sign Mars in a succedent house: taking action, initiating changes with enthusiasm, creating something new via research and development to ensure stability, security, and the preservation of one's identified values. This combination can also be intense, possessive and unyielding as one seeks to transform oneself or the world one inhabits.

Steve Jobs: Mars Birth Resonance Cycle is Pluto

Mars Resonance Cycles After Birth:

1. t.Uranus/Cancer (8/8/55) waxing sq. to Mars (duration only 3+ mo.)

This was the adjustment period (albeit pre-conscious) of his transition from his birth mother to his adoptive parents.

2. t.Neptune/Libra (11/20/55) opp. Mars (duration almost 19 yrs.)

By all accounts, Steve was a clown in school, but his father engaged him in electronics.

1971: Met Steve Wozniac (co-founder of Apple) at age 16.

3. t.Uranus/Libra (11/5/74) opp. Mars (duration 8 yrs.)

1974: Technician job at Atari. Trip to India for 7 months.

He returned to the U.S. changed in appearance (with shaved head).

1976: Wozniac and Jobs founded Apple Computer in Job's family garage. Apple1 sold.

1978: First child, daughter Lisa born with long-time girlfriend.

4. t.Pluto/Libra (12/21/82) opp. Mars (Repeat of Mars Birth Resonance) (duration 12.5 yrs.)

1983: Jobs lured John Sculley away from Pepsi to be CEO of Apple.

1984: Apple introduced the Macintosh computer.

1985: Jobs left Apple after a struggle with the Board of Directors and founded NEXT, a computer platform development company. Met his half-sister for the first time.

1986: Founded Pixar. He remained CEO and majority shareholder until Disney bought it in 2006.

1991: Married Laurene Powell. Son Reed born.

5. t.Uranus/Capricorn (3/6/95) waning sq. to Mars
(duration almost 2 yrs.)

1995: Daughter Erin born.

1997: NEXT was acquired by Apple. Jobs became interim CEO of Apple.

1998: iMac released. Daughter Eve born.

6. t.Neptune/Capricorn (3/3/97) waning sq. to Mars
(duration 14 yrs. 7 mo. until his death)

2000: Full CEO of Apple.

2003: Diagnosed with pancreatic cancer.

2007: Apple entered the cell-phone biz with the i-phone.

Steve Jobs died on 10/5/11 during his *Neptune Resonance Phase.*

The Significance of the "Birth Resonance" Repeating in one's Lifetime

Since you enter this current life with a particular resonance from either Uranus, Neptune or Pluto, this resonance holds a more powerful lesson for you developmentally. You are required to unravel the mystery of this energy, and when this *Planetary Resonance* phase repeats, you have the opportunity to continue that specific developmental lesson and evolve with its message.

CHAPTER 6

Life Trajectory – Mapping the Resonant Influences

The central points of *Planetary Resonance* are as follows. First, there is a lingering effect of the transmissions from the outer three planets that the personality must incorporate, develop and evolve over a span of time or *Resonance Phase*. This effect, development or evolution takes longer than the actual ending of the mathematical transit as we know it. Another point is that there are *mathematical links* (by degree) in every chart that correspond to both the past and to the future – a continuum of energy reaching backwards and forwards in time, to which we are always responding on subtler, background levels.

> *"Classical Astrology has exhausted the astronomical knowledge of its era. It is our task to take up these endeavors, utilizing the modern tools at hand."*
>
> — Theodor Landscheidt, *Cosmic Cybernetics*

Pertaining to the above quote, my belief is that we must evolve astrology to fully include current cosmic and astronomical discoveries, which certainly and primarily include the three outermost planets.

Sequence of Resonance Phases

The sequential order of the contacts made by Uranus, Neptune or Pluto to an inner planet is important to note. It describes the path of development and evolution of the specific personality planet we are exploring -- the "cosmic request" – denoting which of these powerful transforming energies need to be integrated, in which order, and at what particular time in the life.

Note also which *Planetary Resonance Phase* is the **longest** and how that influences the development of a part of the personality.

Case Study of Oprah Winfrey

In this example we'll explore Oprah Winfrey's *Venus Resonance* cycles.

Oprah's Venus is exactly (partile) conjunct her Sun/Aquarius at 9º, which means that they both receive the same *Planetary Resonance* at the same time – throughout her life!

Oprah's Birth Planetary Resonance to Sun/Venus is Pluto/Leo opposite her Sun/Venus Aquarius (exact on 6/12/46). (Duration measured from the birthdate to the next *resonance* is 3 yrs. 7 mo.)

Born to a teenage mother, Oprah went to live with her grandmother as a baby. Raised in rural poverty, her grandmother taught her to read before the age of 3.

Life Trajectory – Mapping the Resonant Influences 41

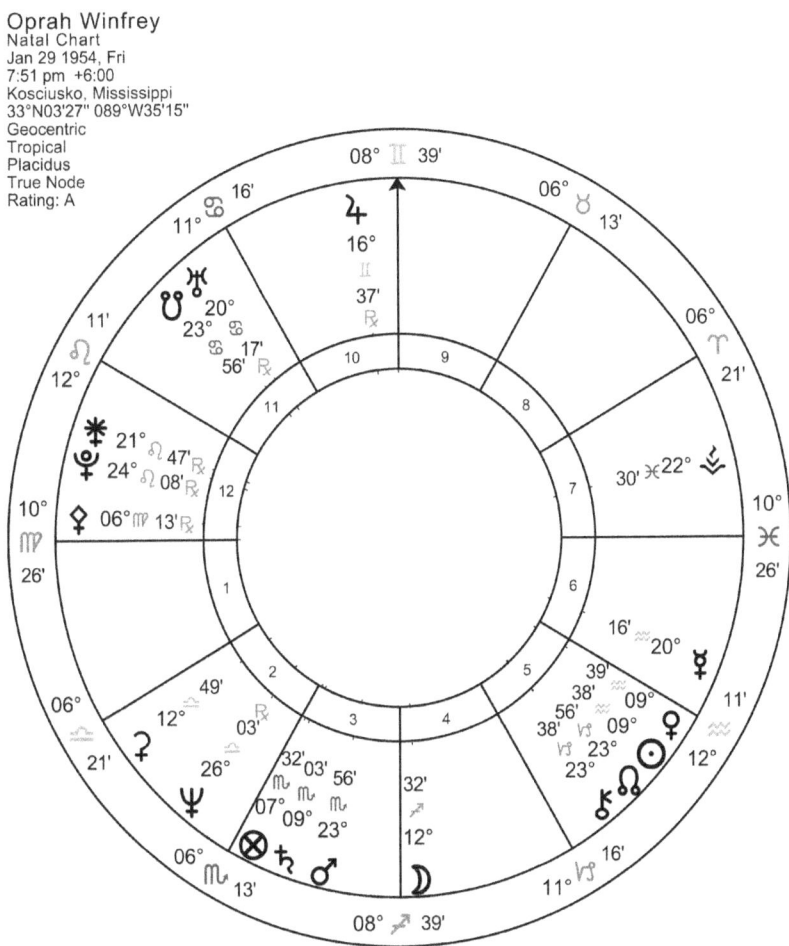

Post-birth *Planetary Resonance Phases* to Oprah's Sun/Venus:

1. t.Uranus/Leo opp. Sun/Venus/Aquarius – 8/29/57
(duration 2.5 yrs)

She was so poor she often wore a potato sack as a dress and was ridiculed for it at school.

2. t.Neptune/Scorpio waning sq. Sun/Venus/Aquarius – 1/19/60 (SR at 9º) (duration 15 yrs. 10 mo)

At age 6, she went back to live with her mother and her half-sister in Milwaukee, WI.

1962: Oprah went to Nashville to live with her father. Her mother gave birth to another daughter.

1963: Age 9--Oprah claimed she began to be sexually abused by a cousin, an uncle and a family friend. She went back to live with mother, who had now given birth to a son.

1967: Age 13--after years of abuse, she ran away from home. Age 14--she became pregnant (her son died shortly after birth).

For High School, she went back to live with her father, who was strict about her education. She thrived and became an honors student, was voted most popular girl and won a scholarship to college. At age 17, she won the Miss Teen Black Tennessee Beauty Pageant.

As a result of her visibility, she was hired as a part-time news anchor for a local black radio station. She held this job from her senior year of high school through the first 2 years of college.

3. t.Uranus/Scorpio waning sq. Sun/Venus/Aquarius – 11/25/76 (duration 10+ yrs).

She moved to Baltimore to co-anchor the 6 o'clock news.

8/14/78: She became co-host of WJZ, a local talk show.

At age 24, she told her family of the sexual abuse she had suffered. They refused to accept it.

9/8/81: She wrote a suicide note over a disastrous love relationship with a married man.

1983: Moved to Chicago to host AM Chicago; first episode aired 1/2/84 and was very successful.

1985: Made the movie The Color Purple (based on the book by Toni Morrison).

9/8/86: The Oprah Winfrey talk show first aired. She became a millionaire at age 32.

Met Stedman Graham, her steady and current partner.

4. t.Pluto/Scorpio waning sq. Sun/Venus/Aquarius – 12/16/86 (duration 11 yrs. 2+ mo)

1986: She told her TV viewers of her sexual abuse during a show on the subject.

1989: Her half-brother died of Aids.

1990: A family member betrayed her by selling the story of her teen pregnancy to The National Enquirer.

1993: She interviewed Michael Jackson on her show before an audience of 36.5 million. It was the most watched television interview ever.

Mid-1990's: Oprah moved from a tabloid news format to a broader range of subject matter.

5. t.Uranus/Aquarius conj. Sun/Venus/Aquarius – 2/3/98 (duration 4 yrs)

Launch of Oprah's philanthropic Angel Network.

6. t.Neptune/Aquarius conj. Sun/Venus/Aquarius – 2/12/02
(duration 18 yrs. 4 mo.)

2002: Received the Bob Hope Humanitarian Award.

2003: Her first half-sister died of cocaine addiction.

2004-2008: Established O, The Oprah Magazine.

2007: In January, Oprah Winfrey Leadership Academy for Girls opened in Johannesburg, South Africa.

1/15/08: Announced plans for OWN (Oprah Winfrey Network)

2010: Oprah learned she has another half-sister who was given up for adoption.

1/1/2011: Launching of OWN.

5/25/11: Oprah Winfrey Show series finale.

7. t.Uranus/Taurus waxing sq. Sun/Venus/Aquarius – 6/10/20
(duration 8 yrs. 8 mo.)

8. t.Pluto/Aquarius conj. Sun/Venus/Aquarius – 2/16/29
(duration 12 yrs. 7+ mo.)

(A return again to her *Birth Resonance*)

9. t.Uranus/Leo opp. Sun/Venus/Aquarius – 8/11/41

What becomes apparent quickly is that after the first *Uranus Planetary Resonance*, which lasted 2.9 years, Oprah had to deal with three sequential squares from planets in Scorpio – first Neptune, then Uranus, and finally Pluto – over the course of 36 years. So, not only are we observing the outer planet *Resonance*, but also the sign the planet is in and the type of aspect it is making. We can say that these years – until Oprah was about 44 years old – were very intense. The Neptune square period were years marked by poverty, neglect, secrets and abuse. The Uranus/Scorpio square brought her sudden advantages and upward movement. Just as Pluto/Scorpio was about to square, The Oprah Winfrey show was launched and she was fully immersed again in her *Pluto Birth Resonance to Sun/Venus*. She became one of the most powerful and influential women in the world during that time.

We can see that the Pluto theme is a dominant one in her chart. This is reinforced by her natal Mars/Scorpio square Pluto/Leo, and her Saturn/Scorpio exactly (partile) square her Sun/Venus/Aquarius! This Pluto theme expresses the need to overcome, to transform and transmute, to rise from the ashes to continue to make one's mark, to maximize one's potentials--and sometimes, as in Oprah's case, to become immensely influential and wealthy. She is an icon. Since 1995, she is the only African American to rank among the 400 richest people in the United States every year.

The fact that Oprah's Sun/Venus conjunction is only minutes apart from exactitude doubles the effect of all the *Planetary Resonance* cycles of her life. Likewise, the exact partile square from Saturn/Scorpio magnifies the effect even more.

Oprah's longest *Planetary Resonance Phase* is from Neptune: 18 years and 4 months. She is currently in this phase. There have been scandals with her school in Johannesburg, and there was also the disclosure of the long-held secret of her half-sister who was given up for adoption. This phase circles back to her early childhood – the period when she endured poverty, neglect and abuse. This adult *Neptune Resonance Phase* appears to be a redemption of sorts: a fulfillment of dreams that were shimmering in the shadowy depths of her unconscious in those earliest years of her life.

CHAPTER 7

The Role of Saturn and Jupiter as Sub-cycles of *Planetary Resonance*

Now that we've explained the basic concept of *Planetary Resonance*, we'll add the sub-cycles of Saturn and Jupiter to the mix for more complexity.

Acceptable astrological principles grant Jupiter and Saturn dominion over the social and cultural realities of the times we are born into and at any given moment in time. So, we will not find the Saturn or Jupiter *Resonance Phases*. This system uses only the five inner planets and the aspects received over a lifetime and the resonance prior to birth, from Uranus, Neptune and Pluto. We are exploring the development of personality, which is represented by the five inner planets.

The Role of Jupiter and Saturn

In short, Saturn and Jupiter represent **Contraction and Expansion** within the larger *Planetary Resonance Phase* we are exploring. They temper or set the tone during a part of the *Resonance Phase* and modify the Uranian, Neptunian or Plutonian energies.

Jupiter and Saturn act like an accordion: opening and closing, breathing in and breathing out. We need those alternate and opposite movements while we are working with and evolving the raw energies of Uranus, Neptune or Pluto.

Saturn keywords: Taming, disciplining, committing or concentrating the energy.

Jupiter keywords: Relaxing, expanding, magnifying or risking the energy.

Jupiter or Saturn will qualify and determine how the larger phase of a Uranus, Neptune or Pluto *Planetary Resonance* cycle will be utilized. Will it have more ease (Jupiter) or will it be more demanding (Saturn)? Will it be expansive or magnified in some sense (Jupiter), or will it be more contractive or narrow in focus (Saturn)?

Because Jupiter has a faster orbital speed, there will be more Jupiter sub-cycles in relation to Saturn sub-cycles in the context of any *Planetary Resonance Phase*. Which means that you'll have more breaks, opportunities and expansion from the demands, focus and pressures delivered by a Saturn sub-cycle during a Uranus, Neptune or Pluto Resonance Phase

Finding a Jupiter or Saturn sub-cycle:

To find the sub-cycles of Jupiter or Saturn, you'll use the same method you used to find the outer planet *Planetary Resonance Phase*.

1. Choose the inner planet you wish to explore.

2. Find the last conjunction, square or opposition made to that planet by Uranus, Neptune or Pluto.

3. Find the last conjunction, square or opposition made to the inner planet of your choice by Jupiter or Saturn.

4. Combine the influence of the *Planetary Resonance Phase* with the influence of the sub-cycle of either Jupiter or Saturn.

Example: Hillary Clinton

Although she is now recognized and admired as a very effective United States Secretary of State, she is also remembered for the scandals of infidelity involving her husband, Bill Clinton, former President of the United States.

We have no verified time of birth for Hillary Clinton (although 8 PM has often been used). Still, we can ascertain a good deal of information using *Planetary Resonance* to examine her Venus—the nature of her relationships and her essential core values—since the degree of Venus will most likely not change in one day.

Hillary Clinton's Birth Planetary Resonance to Venus is Uranus (Uranus/Taurus last opposition to Venus/Scorpio on 4/23/39). This Venus/Uranus Resonance is likely to bring controversy into her relationships, as well as shocks, breaks and unconventionality. In the signs Scorpio/Taurus, we might say betrayals of trust, or issues of self-worth.

Monica Lewinsky/Bill Clinton Sex Scandal:

The Lewinsky/Clinton political sex scandal was first reported in the Drudge Report on 1/17/98. Then the story broke in the Washington Post on 1/21/98.

On 8/17/98 – Bill Clinton admitted to an improper sexual relationship with Monica Lewinsky from November 1995 to March 1997.

12/98 – The US House of Representatives voted to issue Articles of Impeachment. After a 21-day Senate trial, Clinton was acquitted.

50   PLANETARY RESONANCE

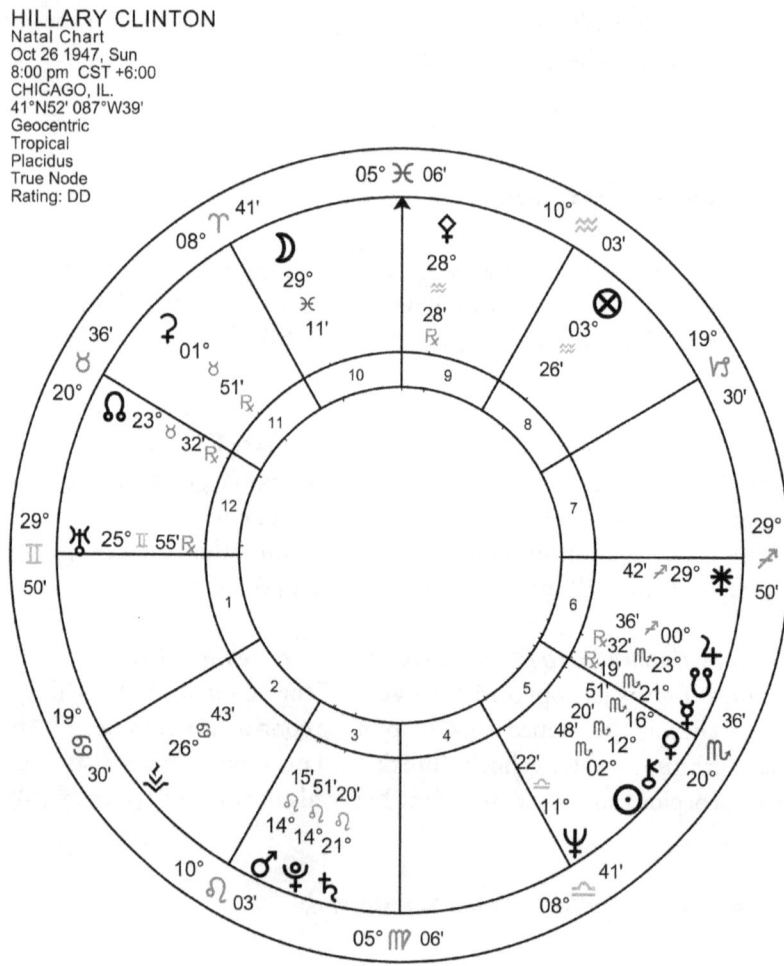

During the time of the scandal, ***Hillary Clinton was in the midst of a Pluto/Venus Resonance Phase*** (since 11/30/89) when Pluto/Scorpio conjoined her Venus/Scorpio.

Consider what was transmitted: Pluto in Scorpio, the raw material of life and death, melding with her natal Venus/Scorpio. She was being asked to take a very deep journey that would require a death of some sort – a need to let go of something, regarding her values and relationships, that would completely transform her previous notions of the quality of relationships, her ability to relate, and even her sense of attractiveness and affection – all functions of Venus. Remember that a conjunction always represents an initiation – both an ending and a new beginning.

Now let's apply the *Saturn/Jupiter sub-cycles.*

Her sub-cycle during the time of the scandal was Saturn, which began when *Saturn/Aquarius squared her Venus/Scorpio* (12/29/92) and lasted until 10/6/94 when *Jupiter/Scorpio conjuncted her Venus/Scorpio* and replaced the Saturn sub-cycle.

This sub-cycle is derived from the last ptolomeic aspect (4th harmonic: conjunction, square or opposition) that was made to her Venus/Scorpio by either Jupiter or Saturn after the *Pluto Resonance Phase to Venus* took effect.

So, we have a combination of Pluto Resonance with Saturn sub-cycle – a combination that's always a forceful pair to be reckoned with. Pluto phases typically bring life/death situations – indelible imprints and transformations that push us to deep levels of marshaling our resources and summoning our power. When the sub-cycle is Saturn, it adds more discipline and demand and often brings a great challenge, with attendant major decisions that must be made amidst great inner turmoil and pressure. The psyche (Pluto) is challenged or tested (Saturn).

Some Events from Hilary Clinton's Venus/Pluto Resonance Phase (1989-1999)

From 1987 to 1991, Hillary Clinton chaired the American Bar Association's Commission on Women in the Profession,

> which addressed gender bias in the law profession and induced the association to adopt measures to combat it. She was first named as one of the 100 most influential lawyers in America by the National Law Journal in 1988 and again in 1991.
>
> Hillary Clinton served on the boards of the Arkansas Children's Hospital Legal Services (1988-1992) and the Children's Defense Fund (as chair, 1986-1992). In addition to her positions with nonprofit organizations, she also held positions on the corporate board of directors of TCBY (1985–1992), Wal-Mart Stores (1986-1992) and Lafarge (1990-1992). Clinton was the first female member on Wal-Mart's board, being invited to sit on the board following pressure on chairman Sam Walton to name a woman to the board. *(Wikipedia)*

Also to be remembered, it was during these years that Bill Clinton was Governor of Arkansas and the intent of the couple clearly was to support and fuel Bill's upward movement in politics. And it was in 1992 that Bill Clinton became the Democratic Presidential Nominee and eventually President of the United States. The majority of the Clinton White House years were during Hillary's Pluto/Venus Resonance. Pluto often invites rises to power and greater empowerment.

> In January 1993, Hillary became First Lady of the United States and was appointed by President Clinton to head the Task Force on National Health Care Reform. The plan was unpopular and was abandoned in late 1994.
>
> Along with Senators Ted Kennedy and Orrin Hatch, she was a force behind the passage of the State Children's Health Insurance Program in 1997, a federal effort that provided state support for children whose parents could not provide them with health coverage.

Together with Attorney General Janet Reno, Clinton helped create the Office on Violence Against Women at the Department of Justice. In 1997, she initiated and shepherded the Adoption and Safe Families Act, which she regarded as her greatest accomplishment as First Lady. *(Wikipedia)*

The Lewinsky scandal dominated 1998.

Clinton traveled to 79 countries during her time as First Lady, breaking the record for most-traveled First Lady (previously held by Pat Nixon).

Hillary Clinton moved into a Venus/Uranus Planetary Resonance Phase (4/8/99). This is a repeat of the *Birth Resonance* to Venus.

Uranus made a Station Retrograde exactly on her Venus at 16° Scorpio on 5/22/99.

This phase signaled the ending of the White House years and heralded new changes in her own political ambitions and relationships.

Clinton was urged to run for an open seat from New York for the United States Senate election of 2000. Once she decided to run, the Clintons purchased a home in Chappaqua, New York, in September 1999. She became the first First Lady of the United States to be a candidate for elected office. Clinton won the election on November 7, 2000, with 55 percent of the vote. She was sworn in as United States Senator on January 3, 2001. *(Wikipedia)*

Now here's yet another interesting way to apply transits of Jupiter and Saturn to one of your inner five planets.

Was it Jupiter or Saturn that made the first contact to your inner planet after your birth?

Which one made the first planetary aspect (again only by conjunction, square or opposition) to one of the five inner planets you've selected to explore? This will tell you whether your first instinctive, pre-conscious imprinting was to be, in general, more cautious or to be more open to risking with regard to the Sun, Moon, Mercury, Venus or Mars.

Knowing whether it was Jupiter or Saturn that made the first contact to your inner five planets will set the tone and bring additional information to the interpretation of the innate quality or essence of the *Birth Resonance Phase* of a particular planet.

For Hillary Clinton's Venus, it was Saturn retrograde in Leo that first contacted her Venus/Scorpio by square, indicating strong relationships and longevity, but many challenges and a general gravitas surrounding her dealings with others. One way we can see that is in her contact with so many people of importance and high visibility, and her own rise to ranks of VIP. Remember when combining these influences that everything must be considered: the planets in signs and houses, as well as the aspect itself.

In Hillary's case we see that this aspect took place in her House 3 and accentuated the powerful square between her stellium of Leo planets and stellium of Scorpio planets. *Planetary Resonance* adds dimension, sometimes reinforcing what is already seen by traditional methods of delineation. At other times it adds more nuance, depth and understanding to the internal and often hidden dynamics at play in the personality.

CHAPTER 8

Using Planetary Resonance

"If you wish to understand the universe, think of energy, frequency and vibration."
— Nikola Tesla

There are five main ways to use *Planetary Resonance* that will give you added dimension and insight into your life or the lives of your clients:

1. Finding the *Birth Planetary Resonance* for each of your five inner planets gives you an understanding of the core transformative and generative energies that are at the root of personality. These are conditions that are sometimes unconscious (below the threshold of awareness), and at other times are reinforced by other aspect configurations in the natal chart, and thereby underscoring a lifelong theme.

2. Finding the *Planetary Resonance* operative in present time for a selected inner planet can shed light on elusive or perplexing, lingering conditions the soul is struggling with, that can sometimes remain unaccounted for with other methods of delineation. If there is one area of life--such as fulfillment or success--that begs more insight, you can look to the *Planetary Resonance* for the Sun to understand which transformative energy is operative and how best to work with it during a given time frame.

For instance, you can work with a client to get a grip on an issue they're dealing with. Assess what a person is most preoccupied with currently. For example, if it is a relationship issue, you would use the planet that describes that issue – Venus for relationship or self-worth – and then apply the *Planetary Resonance* method to that planet. The information revealed is sure to be insightful and useful.

3. Combining #1 and #2: First find the *Birth Planetary Resonance* for your selected inner planet and then find the current *Resonance* for the same planet. Compare them to understand the distinctions between what the person came in primarily to accomplish, the *core resonance,* and what planetary evolution is being asked for now. If the two are the same, as we've stated before, it indicates a pivotal and important phase of life and soul integration that is a core energy for that person.

4. Mapping out your complete lifetime *Planetary Resonance* cycles gives you a unique kind of perspective as to how (and in what sequence and for how long) this life is asking you to develop the intrinsic energy of your birth Sun, Moon, Mercury, Venus or Mars, in relation to the transformative energies of Uranus, Neptune and Pluto.

5. For further clarification as to how best to use each *Resonance Phase,* apply the sub-cycles of Jupiter and Saturn. Is this time contractive/concentrated or expansive/magnified? Is it a time of less or more? Is it a time that has greater flexibility/openness or a time of greater challenge and accountability? Remember that one is not negative and the other positive. Each serves its purpose. (I have seen people pass on during strong Jupiter times – that too is a "journey".) A Saturn sub-phase can provide the discipline and organization you need to get something completed.

So far we have only selected one planet from each of the example charts, found its *Birth Planetary Resonance* and applied subsequent *Resonance Phases* after the actual birth date.

With five inner planets, each one has its own *Birth Resonance* and its lifetime evolution starts from there. Subsequent *Resonance Phases* continue from this core phase.

With that in mind, let's look at Barack Obama's *Birth Resonance* for all of his inner planets and apply some key concepts.

BARACK OBAMA'S *BIRTH RESONANCE*

Obama's Birth Resonance to the Sun – Uranus (Uranus/Leo conjunct the Sun: 6/1/59)

This is an individual who will know controversy early on in life and will need to find the truth and an authentic sense of self within disruption and shocks to consciousness.

Obama's Birth Resonance to the Moon – Pluto (Pluto/Virgo square the Moon: 6/24/60)

Loss and abandonment issues are embedded early on and the feeling life is deep, searching and intense. Early loss of father. Mother was often away due to work. Grandmother was mother substitute. Mother died when he was 34 and she was 52 years old.

Obama's Birth Resonance to Mercury-Neptune (Neptune/Scorpio square Mercury: 9/14/58)

There's an element of the idealist or a deep spiritual and soul searching for the meaning of complex life events. The mind and speech is nuanced, seeks inspiration and can also inspire and enchant others. Enjoys complexity, can be easily misunderstood.

Obama's Birth Resonance to Venus-Uranus (Uranus/Cancer conjunct Venus: 4/28/50)

Many changes in relationships; forced adaptability and awareness of differences; a seeking after truth clarity, and a wider perspective; the need to understand inclusiveness within the diversity of human relations.

Obama's Birth Resonance to Mars-Uranus (Uranus/Gemini square Mars: 6/24/47)

An early knowledge that one is different and does not easily fit in; that one must actively seek or fight for one's identity and the truth of who one is, largely through one's own efforts. Abrupt changes in location or activity.

Some Current *Resonance Phases* for Obama's Planets

In 2012, President Obama is repeating the same Venus Resonance as his *Birth Resonance*: Uranus (the current cycle began on 3/30/11 when Uranus/Aries squared Venus), and he is currently in his Uranus-Mars Birth Resonance (Uranus/Pisces opposite Mars began on 5/18/08). In addition, on 5/12/12, Neptune/Pisces began a new *Planetary Resonance* cycle to his Moon at 3° Gemini. This is reinforced and emphasized by the fact that Neptune makes this square and it is also a station retrograde point. Obama is coming out of a Uranus Planetary Resonance to his Moon which began on 2/26//2004. This current cycle can be a difficult, stressful or confusing time, with a danger of mixed signals and messages – slander and subterfuge. Of course it's election season and there will be lots of smoke and mirrors and hidden agendas, so keeping the record simple and clear will be especially important. We might expect some deep spiritual or inspiring and profound messages emerging in speeches, etc.

Other Important Considerations

1. What are the houses that are involved in *Planetary Resonance* aspects? More than likely, each additional *Resonance Phase* to one of your inner planets will have the same type of house in common.

The transiting aspect will take place in either an angular, succedent or cadent house because we are only using the 4th harmonic aspects. Depending on where the aspect begins, it will always be either a conjunction or a one-quarter turn around the wheel from where it started. If the planet you are examining is in a cadent house, subsequent *Resonance Phases* also take place in cadent houses. *This immediately gives you important information about the inner planet in the chart and the flow of its developmental arena via the houses.*

Briefly, let's discuss the meaning of the types of houses:

Angular Houses (1, 4 ,7, 10): initiating action and greater visibility.

Succedent Houses (2, 5, 8, 11): developing and sustaining

Cadent Houses (3, 6, 9, 12): distributing, flexible

2. It's the same with the Qualities – if you have a fixed Venus in your birth chart, each *Planetary Resonance Phase* to your Venus will be from a fixed outer planet transit aspect.

Cardinal – Action-oriented

Fixed – Determined

Mutable – Adaptable

3. Consider whether the aspect you are receiving is in the *waxing or waning* part of its (natural) cycle in relation to your birth planet. This too will make a difference in interpretation and where you are in the cycle. Waxing planets are taking energy in or building, and waning aspects are sharing or releasing energy. (Think of the phases of the Moon.)

4. Consider what mathematical aspect the outer planet is making to the inner planet: conjunction, square or opposition. This too will

have an affect on your interpretation. A conjunction is always a blending of the two energies, a merging and a brand new beginning in a cycle between those two planets. Squares indicate times of struggle and challenge to the existing status quo, with a need to make decisions. Oppositions are relational and require compromise and balance, as they deal with opposing forces that each demand attention.

5. When your **Birth Planetary Resonance** repeats during your lifetime, this is considered a significant peak time in the energetic development of that part of your personality since the *Birth Resonance* is core to understanding the essential character development of each one of your personal planets.

6. Does one outer planet dominate as a *Birth Resonance*? You are likely to have more Uranus Resonances than those involving Neptune or Pluto. But which one of the inner planets is receiving the Uranian Birth Resonance of awakening, inventiveness, and individuality as its core resonance?

7. Is one of the outer planets missing as a *Birth-Resonance*? We can treat that as we would a missing element: either that vibratory energy was not as necessary to the core development of that planet and/or there is a particular lesson needed from that planetary energy. I've also noted a certain freshness or naivete in approaching the events of that energy when it is missing. And when the missing *Resonance Phase* occurs later in life, that period is likely to be a particularly creative and unique time.

> "Who could deny the validity of Goethe's words: 'My dear friend, all theory is but vagueness'? And yet there is nothing more practical than a good theory. It encompasses all experience gained, illuminates the underlying mutualities, and facilitates predictions which serve to master the future."
>
> — Theodore Landscheidt, *Cosmic Cybernetics*

CHAPTER 9

Calculating Planetary Resonance

Astrology is a number-based system. Its foundation is mathematics. Each number has a distinct vibration and heralds its own "music of the spheres." Over the years, astrologers who are also musicians have formulated a way of translating the numbers in the birth chart to a musical melody.

Planetary Resonance works very specifically with numbers: the degree of each of your inner planets and how they are affected by contacts to those degrees in the past, present and future. It emphasizes the sensitivity of those degrees that belong to a person's natal chart.

> *"The role which the number plays in mythology and in the unconscious provides food for thought. It is one aspect of the physically real as well as of the psychic imagination. It is not only a unit of counting and measuring, it is not merely quantitative in character, it is also a qualitative expression and is therefore a mysterious cross between myth and reality, on the one hand discovered and on the other invented."*
>
> — C.G.Jung

Currently, there is no computer program to calculate all the phases with the sub-phases of *Planetary Resonance*. I hope with the publication of this book, someone will come forward to help program the technique. Since I use Solar Fire, I can explain how to create settings in the Solar Fire Chart calculation program to help you find your basic *Planetary Resonance phases.*

Isolate the inner planet you are using, then create a search for conjunctions, squares or oppositions only, to the target planet over a designated period of time.

In the **Dynamic Reports** tab of Solar Fire, you can create your own parameters. Substitute your own chart in step 1.

1. First bring up a copy of Barack Obama's natal chart.
2. From the **Dynamic Reports** tab, select **Transits and Progressions.** There you can create a new selection in the **Saved Selections** box and name it *Planetary Resonance.*
3. In **Period of Report, choose 100 years.** (This will generate a report for any one of the inner planets you select for hard aspects before birth, or the Birth Resonance, and hard aspects after the birth for those Resonance Phases – all within the 100 year sequence. Begin about 30 years before birth to make sure you capture the last outer planet contact. You can modify the year you begin once you see that the report has calculated and included the last outer planet transit to the inner planet you have chosen.)
4. In the **Location** box, stay with the natal location.
5. In the **Events Selection** box, choose **Transits to Radix**.
6. In the **Dynamic Type** box, do not select anything.
7. In the **Point Selection** box for **Transits,** choose Uranus, Neptune and Pluto. (You will need to either create this or hit the edit button and make sure only those three outer planets are selected and then click SAVE).
8. In the **Point Selection** box for **Radix** (natal planet), choose the planet you want aspected by Uranus, Neptune and Pluto. In the Obama example, we've selected Mars.
9. In the **Aspect Selection** box, choose conjunction, square opposi-

Calculating Planetary Resonance   63

tion only. Edit the orbs for the aspects so that they are **exact orbs** (this will then generate the date the aspect is exact, which is what we want).

Here is the screen shot of what was explained above.

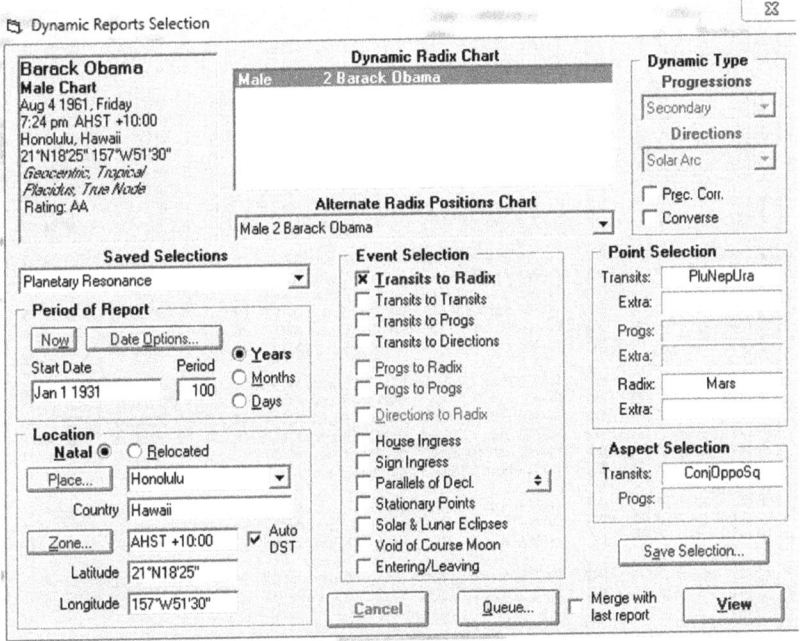

Following is the Dynamic Report generated using the Solar Fire Dynamic Report screen for transits to Obama's Mars position before and after his birth. Once the report is generated, you can easily see which of the outer three planets was the one to make the last (closest) 4th harmonic aspect before birth. In Obama's Dynamic Report, I've highlighted the closest outer planet transit to Obama's Mars position of 22° Virgo before his birth which is Uranus/Gemini square his Mars/Virgo.

Dynamic Events Report

Dynamic Chart (2):
Barack Obama - Male Chart
Aug 4 1961, 7:24 pm, AHST +10:00
Honolulu Hawaii, 21°N18'25", 157°W51'30"
Geocentric Tropical Zodiac
Placidus Houses, True Node

P1 (H)	Asp	P2 (H)	EXL	Type	Date	Time	Zone	Age	Pos1	Pos2
♆ (7)	☌	♂ (7)	(X)	Tr-Na	Nov 3 1938	00:17:55 am	HST	-22.754	22°♍34' D	22°♍34' D
♆ (7)	☌	♂ (7)	(X)	Tr-Na	Feb 18 1939	05:02:52 am	HST	-22.461	22°♍34' ℞	22°♍34' D
♆ (7)	☌	♂ (7)	(X)	Tr-Na	Sep 3 1939	03:15:03 am	HST	-21.921	22°♍34' D	22°♍34' D
♅ (4)	□	♂ (7)	(X)	Tr-Na	Jun 24 1947	10:47:00 am	AHST	-14.115	22°♊34' D	22°♍34' D
♅ (4)	□	♂ (7)	(X)	Tr-Na	Jan 27 1948	05:13:07 am	AHST	-13.521	22°♊34' ℞	22°♍34' D
♅ (4)	□	♂ (7)	(X)	Tr-Na	Apr 1 1948	06:17:31 pm	AHST	-13.342	22°♊34' D	22°♍34' D
♅ (7)	☌	♂ (7)	(X)	Tr-Na	Oct 25 1966	08:23:55 pm	AHST	5.224	22°♍34' D	22°♍34' D
♅ (7)	☌	♂ (7)	(X)	Tr-Na	Mar 8 1967	08:36:45 pm	AHST	5.591	22°♍34' ℞	22°♍34' D
♅ (7)	☌	♂ (7)	(X)	Tr-Na	Aug 11 1967	07:56:06 pm	AHST	6.018	22°♍34' D	22°♍34' D
♇ (7)	☌	♂ (7)	(X)	Tr-Na	Nov 23 1967	05:01:44 pm	AHST	6.302	22°♍34' D	22°♍34' D
♇ (7)	☌	♂ (7)	(X)	Tr-Na	Jan 27 1968	11:39:33 am	AHST	6.480	22°♍34' ℞	22°♍34' D
♇ (7)	☌	♂ (7)	(X)	Tr-Na	Sep 12 1968	11:45:55 am	AHST	7.107	22°♍34' D	22°♍34' D
♇ (7)	☌	♂ (7)	(X)	Tr-Na	May 7 1969	06:17:18 pm	AHST	7.756	22°♍34' ℞	22°♍34' D
♇ (7)	☌	♂ (7)	(X)	Tr-Na	Jun 27 1969	10:43:01 am	AHST	7.895	22°♍34' D	22°♍34' D
♆ (10)	□	♂ (7)	(X)	Tr-Na	Mar 5 1980	11:33:37 am	AHST	18.584	22°♐34' D	22°♍34' D
♆ (10)	□	♂ (7)	(X)	Tr-Na	Apr 12 1980	10:47:24 am	AHST	18.688	22°♐34' ℞	22°♍34' D
♆ (10)	□	♂ (7)	(X)	Tr-Na	Dec 18 1980	06:53:38 pm	AHST	19.373	22°♐34' D	22°♍34' D
♆ (10)	□	♂ (7)	(X)	Tr-Na	Jul 20 1981	06:02:12 pm	AHST	19.959	22°♐34' ℞	22°♍34' D
♆ (10)	□	♂ (7)	(X)	Tr-Na	Oct 15 1981	05:45:21 pm	AHST	20.197	22°♐34' D	22°♍34' D
♅ (10)	□	♂ (7)	(X)	Tr-Na	Dec 14 1986	02:55:06 pm	AHST	25.361	22°♐34' D	22°♍34' D
♇ (10)	□	♂ (7)	(X)	Tr-Na	Dec 27 2004	01:17:33 pm	AHST	43.398	22°♐34' D	22°♍34' D
♇ (10)	□	♂ (7)	(X)	Tr-Na	Jul 7 2005	09:14:06 am	AHST	43.923	22°♐34' ℞	22°♍34' D
♇ (10)	□	♂ (7)	(X)	Tr-Na	Oct 25 2005	05:24:11 pm	AHST	44.225	22°♐34' D	22°♍34' D
♅ (1)	☍	♂ (7)	(X)	Tr-Na	Jun 12 2008	01:05:48 pm	AHST	46.856	22°♓34' D	22°♍34' D
♅ (1)	☍	♂ (7)	(X)	Tr-Na	Jul 10 2008	05:45:51 pm	AHST	46.933	22°♓34' ℞	22°♍34' D
♅ (1)	☍	♂ (7)	(X)	Tr-Na	Mar 12 2009	03:06:38 am	AHST	47.602	22°♓34' D	22°♍34' D
♆ (1)	☍	♂ (7)	(X)	Tr-Na	May 7 2021	06:00:42 pm	AHST	59.757	22°♓34' D	22°♍34' D
♆ (1)	☍	♂ (7)	(X)	Tr-Na	Aug 14 2021	12:08:02 pm	AHST	60.028	22°♓34' ℞	22°♍34' D
♆ (1)	☍	♂ (7)	(X)	Tr-Na	Mar 5 2022	05:51:42 am	AHST	60.583	22°♓34' D	22°♍34' D
♅ (4)	□	♂ (7)	(X)	Tr-Na	Aug 31 2030	06:48:25 pm	AHST	69.075	22°♊34' D	22°♍34' D
♅ (4)	□	♂ (7)	(X)	Tr-Na	Oct 25 2030	07:56:15 am	AHST	69.224	22°♊34' ℞	22°♍34' D

The report will also show you how many hits each of the outer planets made in a particular *Resonance Phase,* which also indicates the potency of the cycle.

Now you can alter the Dynamic Report to include the Jupiter and Saturn sub-phases, but I would suggest working with the *Resonance* phases of Uranus, Neptune and Pluto first.

Alternatively, using the old-fashioned way, with a bit of time and persistence, you can always find your *Planetary Resonance* cycles by thumbing through the ephemeris until you reach the date when a hard aspect took place for your *Birth Resonance* going backwards from the birth date. Or, for present time, the last hard aspect to the inner planet you are seeking to delineate. And for the future, the next hard aspect transit to your selected inner planet. The computer generated report is, of course, faster! Still, there is something to be said for thumbing through the ephemeris and observing how the planets are moving in relation to your inner planet. It provides a very different experience.

CHAPTER 10

More Examples: Public Figures/Event

Barack Obama, Michael Jackson, Mark Zuckerberg, Facebook, Anais Nin.

This section gives you an opportunity to look at complete cycles and application of the *Planetary Resonance* phases to these individuals and one event of note.

NOTE: The following abbreviations are used in all Planetary Resonance Case Study Examples.

t. = Transit
SR = Stationary Retrograde, SD = Stationary Direct
For Aspects: conj. = conjunction; sq. = square; opp = opposition
For House positions: House 7 becomes H7

BARACK OBAMA: 8/4/61 at 7:24 PM, Honolulu, HI (RatingAA: from Birth Certificate)

Barack Obama's Mars Resonance Cycle

He is born resonating with Uranus to Mars

Uranus in relation to Mars represents the unusual, individualistic, disruptive, shocks, separations from male/father and separations in general; the need to independently form identity, recognition of being different, unconventional, a need for freedom.

Birth UR/MA Resonance lasts from 8/4/61-10/16/66 (duration 5 yrs. 2 mo.)

Parents divorced, mother met and married Indonesian man.

First Resonance after birth is same as Birth Resonance!

This is significant and emphasizes the energy of Uranus as a stimulant to his Mars/male and initiatory identity.

1. t.Uranus/Virgo conj. Mars/Virgo (H7) - 10/25/66 at age 5 yrs. 2 mo. (duration 1 yr.)

Moved to Indonesia.

2. t.Pluto/Virgo conj. Mars/Virgo (H7) – 11/23/67 at age 6 yrs. 3 mo. (duration 13 yrs.)

Sister Maya born, moved back to HI, lived with grandparents, met birth father (for first and only time), moved to L.A.

3. t.Neptune/Sag. sq. Mars/Virgo (H10) – 3/5/80 at age 19 yrs. 5 mo. (duration 6+ yrs.)

Transferred to Columbia University in NYC, father died in car accident, graduated from Columbia.

4. t.Uranus/Sag. sq. Mars/Virgo (H10) – 12/14/86 at age 25 yrs. 4 mo. (duration 17+ yrs.)

More Examples: Public Figures/Event 69

First trip to Europe/Kenya, entered Harvard Law School, book published, elected to Illinois Senate, elected to US Senate, married Michelle, mother died, 2 daughters born.

5. t.Pluto/Sag. sq. Mars/Virgo (H10) – 12/27/04 at age 43 yrs. 4 mo. (duration 3.5 yrs.)

Return to Kenya (second time), announced candidacy for President.

6. t.Uranus/Pisces opp. Mars/Virgo (H1) – 6/12/08 at age 46 yrs. 10 mo. (duration 12 yrs. 11 mo.)

Elected President of US, won Nobel Prize for Peace.

7. t.Neptune/Pisces opp. Mars/Virgo (H1) – 5/7/21 at age 59 yrs. 8 mo.

Barack Obama's Mars Resonance Cycle including Jupiter and Saturn

The following is an expansion of Obama's Mars Resonance cycle including the sub-cycles of Jupiter and Saturn.

Obama is born resonating with Uranus to Mars.

Birth Uranus/Mars Resonance lasts from 8/4/61-10/25/66 (duration 5 yrs. 2 mo.)

Sub-cycles:
t.Jupiter/Pisces opp. Mars/Virgo – 3/63
t.Jupiter/Gemini sq. Mars/Virgo – 7/65
t.Saturn/Pisces opp. Mars/Virgo – 3/66
Separation/divorce of birth parents.

Mother met and married Indonesian man.

First Resonance change after birth is same as Birth Resonance!

1. t.Uranus/Virgo conj. Mars/Virgo – 10/25/66
at age 5 yrs. 2 mo. (duration 1 yr.)

Sub-cycle still active: t.SA/PI opp. MA/VI

1967 - Moved to Indonesia (age 6-10)

**2. t.Pluto/Virgo conj. Mars/Virgo – 11/23/67
at age 6 yrs. 3 mo. (duration 13 yrs.)**

Starts with Saturn/Pisces sub-cycle – opp.

t.Jupiter/Virgo sub-cycle on 10/6/68 – conj.
1970 – Half-sister Maya born 8/15/70
t.Jupiter/Sagittarius 12/31/71 – sq.

1971 – Moved back to Hawaii to live with grandparents (Grade 5 through High School).

*Met his birth father for the first and only time in Hawaii (1 month).

1972 – Obama's mother returned to Hawaii to live.

t.Saturn/Gemini 5/30/73 – sq.
t.Jupiter/Pisces   2/13/75 – opp.
t.Jupiter/Gemini 7/12/77 – sq.

1977 – Obama's mother returned to Indonesia as anthropological field worker.

t.Saturn/Virgo 10/20/79 – conj.

1979 – Obama moved to L.A. to attend Occidental College.

3. t.Neptune/Sagittarius sq. Mars/Virgo – 3/5/80 (duration 6+ yrs.)

t.Saturn/Gemini sub-cycle
t.Jupiter/Virgo on 9/20/80 – conj.

1981 – Obama gave his first public speech, fall 1981; transferred to Columbia in NYC.

1982 – Father died in car accident in Kenya.

t.Jupiter/Sagittarius 12/15/83 – sq.

1983 – Graduation from Columbia in Political Science/International Relations.

1985 – Began work as community organizer in Chicago's South Side until 1988.

4. t.Uranus/Sagittarius sq. Mars/Virgo – 3/5/80 (duration 17+ yrs.)

t.Jupiter/Sagittarius sub-cycle – sq.
t.Jupiter/Pisces 6/20/86 – opp.
t.Saturn/Sagittarius 12/3/87 – sq.

1988 (mid) – First trip to Europe and Kenya

1988 – Entered Harvard Law School

t.Jupiter/Gemini 6/25/89 – sq.

June 1989 – Met his future wife, Michelle Robinson

1991 – Accepted 2 year term as visiting law and government fellow at University of Chicago Law School.

1995 – Mother died

5. t.Pluto/Sagittarius sq. Mars/Virgo – 12/27/04 (duration 3.5 yrs.)

t.Saturn/Gemini sub-cycle

2006 – Returned to Kenya (second time)

2/10/07 – Announced his candidacy for Presidency

t.Jupiter/Sagittarius 11/13/07

6. t.Uranus/Pisces opp. Mars/Virgo – 6/12/08 (duration 1 yr. 10 mo.)

t.Jupiter/Sagittarius sub-cycle – sq.

Elected 44th President of the United States – 11/08

t.Saturn/Virgo 8/25/09 – conj.

10/9/09 – Won Nobel Peace Prize

3/21//10 – Health Care Bill signed

t.Jupiter/Pisces 4/14/10 – opp.
t.Jupiter/Gemini 5/22/13 – sq.
t.Jupiter/Virgo 12/11/15 – conj.
t.Saturn/Sagittarius 1/7/17 – sq.

7. t. Neptune/Pisces opp. Mars/Virgo – 5/7/21

t.Jupiter/Sagittarius sub-cycle, change to Jupiter/Pisces 4/4/22
t.Saturn/Pisces 3/12/2 - opp.
t.Jupiter/Gemini 5/5/25 - sq.

More Examples: Public Figures/Event 73

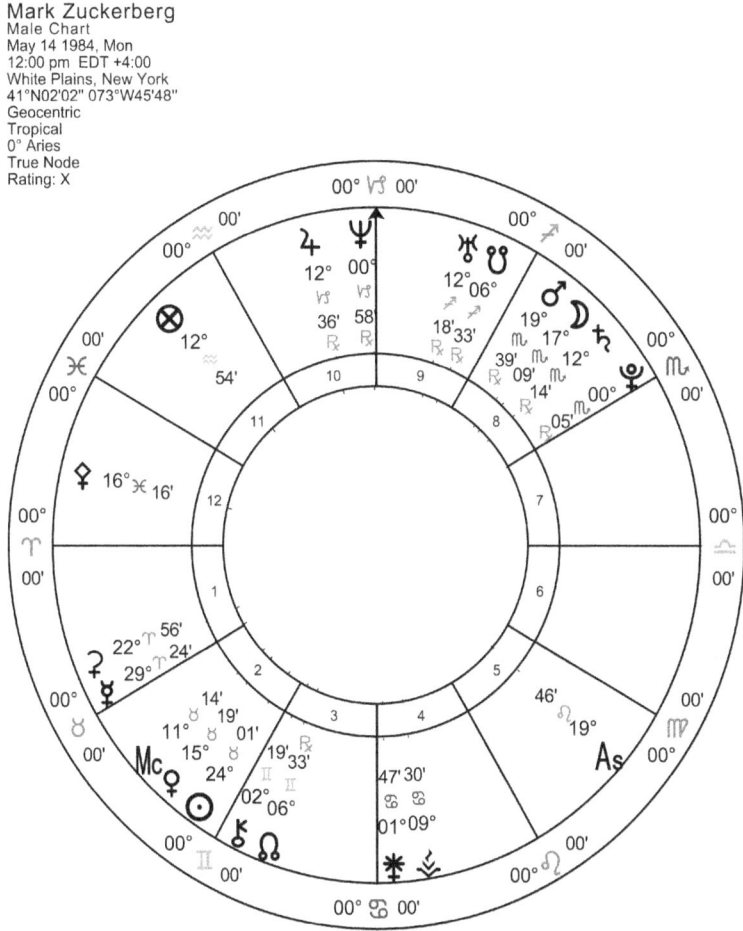

Mark Zuckerberg, Creator of Facebook

Birth Data: 5/14/84, White Plains, NY (RR: X, time unknown)

Mark Elliot Zuckerberg: Computer programmer and Internet entrepreneur. He is best known for co-creating the social networking site Facebook, of which he is Chief Executive. It was co-founded as a private company in 2004 by Zuckerberg and classmates Dustin

Moskovitz, Eduardo Saverin, and Chris Hughes while they were students at Harvard University. Zuckerberg was named four times in Time 100: in 2009 as one of the 100 most influential people of the world, in 2010 as Time magazine's Person of the Year, in 2011 as one of the 100 most influential people of the world, and in 2012 in "The All-Time TIME 100 of All Time" by Joel Stein in Time. As of 2011, his personal wealth was estimated to be $17.5 billion making him one of the world's youngest billionaires.

Born with Mars 19° Scorpio

Mars Birth Planetary Resonance is Uranus/Scorpio conj. Mars 10/7/79 (duration 6 yrs. 7 mo.)

Unusual, inventive, loner, brilliant

t.Saturn/Scorpio conj. Mars – 11/84
t.Jupiter/Aquarius sq. Mars – 1/86
t.Jupiter/Taurus opp. Mars – 5/88

1. t.Pluto/Scorpio conj. Mars on 12/14/90 (age 6 yrs. 7 mo.)
(duration 15 yrs. 3.5 mo.)

t.Jupiter/Leo sq. Mars – 7/91
t.Saturn/Aquarius sq. Mars – 1/93
t.Jupiter/Scorpio conj.Mars – 1/94
t.Jupiter/Aquarius sq. Mars – 4/97
t.Saturn/Taurus opp. Mars – 4/00
t.Jupiter/Taurus opp. Mars – 5/00
t.Jupiter/Leo sq. Mars – 7/03

Facebook was launched here:
Pluto Resonance and Jupiter sub-cycle – 2/4/04

2. t.Neptune/Aquarius sq. Mars on 3/28/06 (nearly 22 yrs. old) (duration 17 yrs.)

Facebook goes wildly viral and becomes number one social hotspot

t.Saturn/Leo sq. Mars – 9/06
t.Jupiter/Aquarius sq. Mars – 4/09
t.Jupiter/Taurus opp. Mars – 4/12
Impending IPO announced
t.Saturn/Scorpio conj. Mars – 12/13

3. t.Uranus/Taurus opp. Mars on 5/11/23 (nearly 40 yrs. old)

Birth planetary resonance repeats.

76 PLANETARY RESONANCE

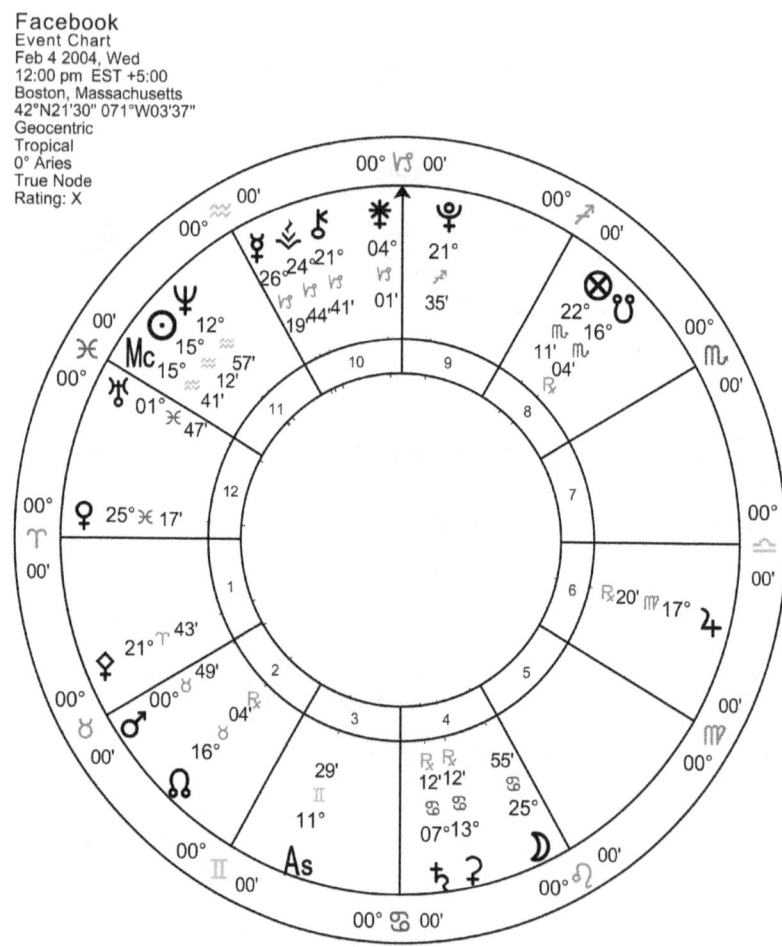

Facebook 2/4/04, Boston, MA (RR: X—Time Unknown)

Mars Birth Resonance: Mars at 0° Taurus

Neptune 0° Aquarius 12/30/98 sq. Mars/Taurus (duration 20 yrs.)

Facebook launched 2/4/04

t.Saturn/Leo sq. Mars/Taurus – 7/17/05
t.Jupiter/Scorpio opp. Mars/Taurus – 10/27/05
t.Jupiter/Aquarius sq. Mars/Taurus – 1/6/09
t.Jupiter/Taurus conj. Mars/Taurus – 6/5/11
t.Saturn/Scorpio opp. Mars/Taurus – 10/5/12
t.Jupiter/Leo sq. Mars/Taurus – 7/17/14

1. t.Uranus 0° Taurus 5/16/18 conj. Mars/Taurus

Facebook's Mars Birth Resonance lasts for 20 years! We can certainly say that Neptune would be considered viral, dissolving boundaries. It will be interesting what happens in 2018 at the first Mars Resonance after its launch.

Michael Jackson

Birth Data: August 29, 1958 7:33 PM Gary, Indiana. (RR: DD Time from Jackson to Chakrapani Ullal via Stephen Stuckey – not completely verified). Aries wheel used.

(NOTE: The following biographical material is excerpted from Wikipedia)

Michael Joseph Jackson: American recording artist, entertainer, and businessman. Often referred to as the King of Pop. Jackson is recognized as the most successful entertainer of all time by Guinness World Records. His contribution to music, dance, and fashion, along with a much-publicized personal life, made him a global figure in popular culture for over four decades. The seventh child of the Jackson family, he debuted on the professional music scene along with his brothers as a member of The Jackson 5 in 1964, and began his solo career in 1971.

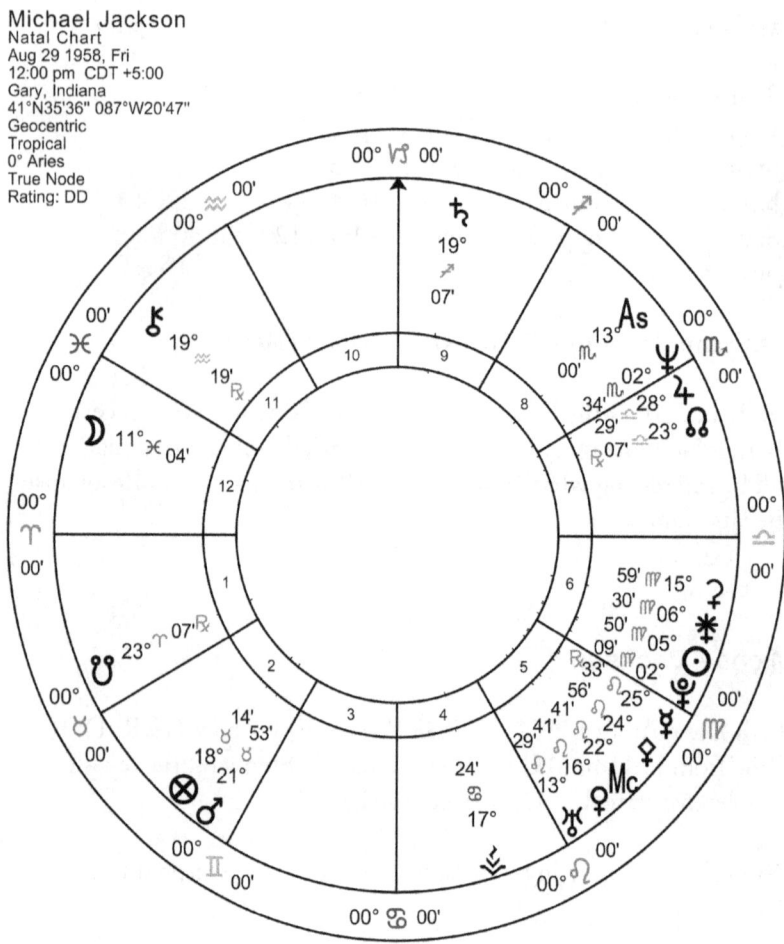

In the early 1980s, Jackson became a dominant figure in popular music. The music videos for his songs, including those of "Beat It," "Billie Jean," and "Thriller," were credited with transforming the medium into an art form and a promotional tool, and the popularity of these videos helped to bring the relatively new television channel MTV to fame. Through stage performances and music videos, Jackson popularized a number of complicated dance techniques.

Jackson's 1982 album *Thriller* is the best-selling album of all time. Jackson won hundreds of awards, which made him the most-awarded recording artist in the history of popular music. He was also one of the world's most prominent humanitarians and philanthropists; personally, and through his Heal the World Foundation, he donated more than 300 million dollars to charity. Aspects of Jackson's personal life, including his changing appearance, personal relationships, and behavior, generated controversy. In 1993, he was accused of child sexual abuse, but the case was settled out of court and no formal charges were brought. In 2005, he was tried and acquitted of further child sexual abuse allegations. While preparing for his latest concert, *This Is It*, Jackson died of acute propofol and benzodiazepine intoxication on June 25, 2009. The Los Angeles County Coroner ruled his death a homicide, and his personal physician was convicted of involuntary manslaughter.

Venus Planetary Resonance Phases:
Venus at 16º Leo – Venus Birth Resonance Phase: Pluto/Leo conj. Venus (May 1950)

1. t.Uranus/Leo conj. Venus – 10/58; SR at 16º– 11/58 (duration 5+ years)
t.Jupiter/Scorpio sq. – 11/58
t.Jupiter/Aquarius opp. – 1/62
t.Saturn/Aquarius opp. – 2/63

2. t.Neptune/Scorpio sq. Venus – 11/63 (duration 13+ yrs.)
t.Jupiter/Taurus sq. – 6/64, SD at 16º, 1/11/65
t.Jupiter/Leo conj. – 8/67
t.Saturn/Taurus sq. – 6/70, 12/70
t.Jupiter/Scorpio sq. – 12/70
t.Jupiter/Aquarius opp. – 1/74
t.Jupiter/Taurus sq. – 6/76
t.Saturn/Leo conj. – 10/76, SR at 16º, 7/77

3. t.Uranus/Scorpio sq. Venus – 1/78; SR at 16°–2/78; SD at 16°–7/79 (duration 10+ yrs.)
t.Jupiter/Leo conj. – 7/79
t.Jupiter/Scorpio sq. – 10/82
t.Saturn/Scorpio sq. – 2/84, SR at 16°–10/84
t.Jupiter/Aquarius opp. – 5/85, SR at 16°–12/85
t.Jupiter/Taurus sq. – 5/88

4. t.Pluto/Scorpio sq. – 12/89 (duration 10+ yrs.)
t.Jupiter/Leo conj. – 7/91
t.Saturn/Aquarius opp. – 4/92
t.Jupiter/Scorpio sq. – 10/94
t.Jupiter/Aquarius opp. – 4/97

5. t.Uranus/Aquarius opp. – 4/99, SR at 16°– 5/99; SD at 16°– 10/00 (duration 8.5 yrs.)
t..Saturn/Taurus sq. – 7/99
t.Jupiter/Taurus sq. – 5/00
t.Jupiter/Leo conj. – 10/02

6. t.Neptune/Aquarius opp. – 3/05 (duration 4.5 yrs.)
t.Jupiter/Scorpio sq. – 1/06
t.Saturn/Leo conj. – 8/06
t.Jupiter/Aquarius opp. – 3/09

Michael Jackson died on June 25, 2009, at age 50, of propofol intoxication after suffering a respiratory arrest at his home in Los Angeles. Jackson died during a Venus/Neptune Resonance Phase with a Jupiter sub-cycle. This clearly fits a drug overdose.

More Examples: Public Figures/Event 81

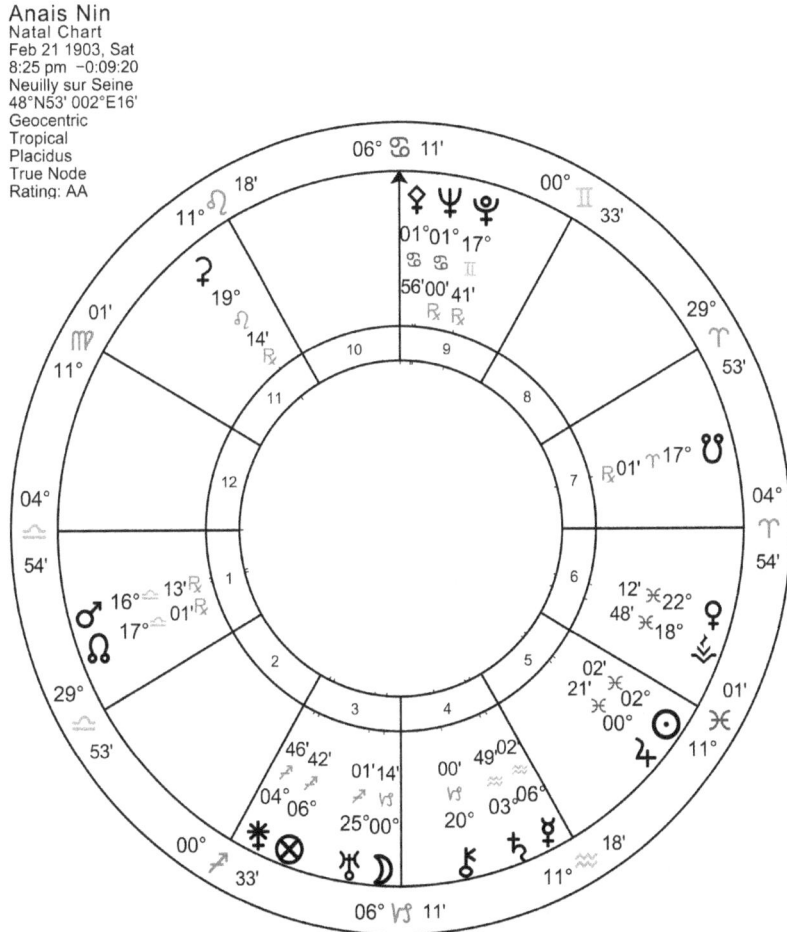

Anais Nin

Birth Data: 2/21/1903 8:00 PM, Neuilly sur Seine, France
(RR: AA)

Although controversial, I've included Anais Nin precisely for that reason. She was a woman ahead of her time who helped to bring the unique emotional life and perspective of women to light.

(NOTE: The following biographical material is excerpted from Wikipedia.)

French writer who authored 60 diaries in her 74 years about her SELF (often capitalized), she began her diaries at 15. She became an icon for the feminist movement in the 1970s, presenting herself as having successfully defied the conventions of woman's traditional role. She was among the first to write of personal explorations about sex, self and psychoanalysis. Her marriages and affairs were detailed in her books.

Her dad was the philandering Spanish composer, Joaquin Nin, who abandoned the family when she was 11 but continued to be the overshadowing figure in her life. She was among the first to explore in print three of this century's biggest preoccupations: sex, the self and psychoanalysis. Nin's emphasis on the intimate, personal and instinctual were feminine traits she believed could be used in the reconstruction of a more sensitive world. Her first book, published when she was 27, was about D.H. Lawrence with whom she agreed that lies were essential because most people could not stomach the naked truth. She would brag about lying "bravely, ironically, dually, triply."

Nin clung obsessively to the book that nourished her living; her diary, her "one true friend." She kept both real and false diaries, editing and rewriting them throughout her life in a never-ending recreation of self. In 1933 after a separation of nearly 20 years, she met and seduced her own father who was then 54.

Quixotic in her choice of lovers, Nin was pragmatic when it came to husbands. Both husbands were steadfast men who gave her unstinting support. In 1923 she married a banker, Hugh Guiler, called "Hugo." Hugo paid for the publication of many of her books and made possible the glamorous, art-infested life she led. He turned a blind eye to her love affairs with Henry Miller and her psychoanalysts. In 1934 she became pregnant, the first of several subsequent aborted pregnancies.

She aborted her six-month old, stillborn daughter and fictionalized the event in "Under a Glass Bell." In 1955 she married Rupert Pole bigamously for she had not divorced Hugo.

Venus at 22° Pisces in H 6

Venus Birth Resonance Cycle: Uranus at 22° Sagittarius sq. Venus (12/23/02)

1. t.Uranus/Sagittarius Rx sq. Venus – 7/03 (duration 2 yrs.)

Disruption/stress between parents in the early home environment

2. t.Pluto/Gemini sq. Venus – 7/05, SR at 22°– 9/05, SD at 22°– 3/08 (duration 17 yrs.)

2 brothers born. Almost died twice – typhoid fever, appendicitis

Married Hugo Guiler against his parent's wishes, who disinherited him.

3. t.Uranus/Pisces conj. Venus – 3/25 (duration 12 yrs.)

Moved to Paris 8/25. Many cultural events, first affair with dance teacher.

Intense sexual experimentation, many affairs, most notable with the writer Henry Miller. Also, incestuous relationship with her father.

4. t.Neptune/Virgo opp. Venus – 10/38 (duration 9 yrs.)

Began serious writing, published a book. Moved to NY.

5. t.Uranus/Gemini sq. Venus – 6/47, SD at 22°– 3/48 (duration 19 yrs.)

Met Rupert Pole in 1947. Began leading a double life in New York and California, full of lies. She remained married to Hugo Guiler, simultaneous relationship with Pole, whom she married in March 1955.

6. t.Uranus/Virgo opp. Venus – 10/66 (duration 1 yr.)

First volume of diaries published. She is now famous with many interviews and lectures. Filed for an annulment from Rupert, as she was still married to Hugo.

7. t.Pluto/Virgo opp. Venus – 10/67, SR at 22°–12/67, SD at 22°–7/69

Anais contracted vaginal cancer in 1969. Radiation followed from 1970-73.

The LA Times named her "Woman of the Year" in 1976.

Anais Nin died on 1/14/77 at 1:55 PM in NYC, in a Pluto resonance cycle.

Anais Nin Venus Planetary Resonance Phases with Jupiter/Saturn sub-cycle:

Birth Venus at 22° Pisces in H6

Venus Birth Resonance Cycle: Uranus at 22° Sagittarius sq. Venus

1. t.Uranus/Sagittarius Rx sq. Venus – 7/03 (duration 2 yrs.)

(t.Jupiter/Pisces conj. – 6/03, 8/03, 1/04)

2. **t.Pluto/Gemini sq.Venus − 7/05, SD at 22°− 9/05; SD at 22°− 3/08 (duration 17 yrs.)**

t.Jupiter/Gemini sq. − 6/06
t.Saturn/Pisces conj. − 4/07
t.Jupiter/Virgo opp. − 9/09
t.Jupiter/Sagittarius sq. − 12/12
t.Saturn/Gemini sq. − 6/14
t.Jupiter/Pisces − 5/15
t.Jupiter/Gemini − 6/18
t.Saturn/Virgo opp. − 11/20
t.Jupiter/Virgo opposition − 8/21
t.Jupiter/Sagittarius square − 11/24

3. **t.Uranus/Pisces conj. Venus − 3/25 (duration 12 yrs.)**

t.Jupiter/Pisces − 4/27
t.Saturn/Sagittarius − 12/28
t.Jupiter/Gemini − 5/30
t.Jupiter/Virgo − 12/32
t.Jupiter/Sagittarius − 3/36
t..Saturn/Pisces conj. − 6/36 −SD at 22° − 7/36

4. **t.Neptune/Virgo opp. Venus − 10/38**

t..Jupiter/Pisces conj. − 4/39
t..Jupiter/Gemini sq. − 5/42
t..Saturn/Gemini sq. − 8/43
t..Jupiter/Virgo opp. − 11/44

5. **t.Uranus/Gemini sq. Venus − 6/47, SD at 22°− 3/48**

t..Jupiter/Sagittarius sq. − 2/48
t..Saturn/Virgo opp. − 9/50
t..Jupiter/Pisces conj. − 3/51
t..Jupiter/Gemini sq. − 8/53

t..Jupiter/Virgo opp. – 10/56
t..Saturn/Sagittarius sq. – 1/58
t..Jupiter/Sagittarius – 1/60
t..Jupiter/Pisces – 3/63

t..Jupiter/Gemini sq. – 7/65
t..Saturn/Pisces conj. – 3/66, SD at 22° – 11/66

6. t.Uranus/Virgo opp. Venus – 10/66

7. t.Pluto/Virgo opp. Venus – 10/67, SR at 22°–12/67, SD at 22°–7/69

t..Jupiter/Virgo sq. – 10/68
t..Jupiter/Sagittarius sq. – 1/72
t..Saturn/Sagittarius sq. – 6/73
t..Jupiter/Pisces conj. – 2/75

NOTE: If you run computer reports for the examples given in this book, you may find some date discrepancies. This is due to the fact that some of the aspects were not calculated via computer; rather, the first partile (numerical) contact was used without the exact minutes of the degree. Actually there is room and reason to consider both ways to calculate and it can be a personal mini-research for you, while you are already experimenting with this method! It does not change the interpretation of the *Resonance Phase* in any way, but the timing may differ by a month (more or less). What I deem most important is the power of the actual "number" or degree that we are analyzing.

"In the Olympic host, the eternal number reigns supreme. My intention here…is to show that the juxtaposition of the human world and the transcendental world is not absolute but, at the most, relatively incommensurable, the link between Here and Beyond is not entirely lacking. In between is namely the great mediary, the number, whose reality is equally valid here and there, an archetype of its own being."

— Carl Jacobi, German Mathematician

Want to learn more about Planetary Resonance?

Ongoing Group-Coaching for astrologers.

Join a monthly 45-minute group Conference Call for $15

Limited to 10 students.

Contact Dorothy for info to join: DOja07@gmail.com

(fee valid through 12/31/12)

MINDWORKS — Dorothy Oja

Let me help you manage your planets!

Dorothy is a career astrologer, teacher, lecturer and writer. Her practice, MINDWORKS, offers: Timing and Electional work (dates for surgery, weddings, business openings, etc.), Composite/Davison Relationship and Couples analysis, Children's Profiles, and private tutoring. An active writer, Dorothy has written dozens of articles for national magazines and online sites. She has published PlanetWeather ezine for the past 15 years, which interprets planetary patterns and includes social, cultural and political commentary. Additionally, she has hosted her own radio shows, frequently appeared as a guest on TV and interviewed in the print media. Dorothy published Compatibility & Conflict for Romantic Relationships as a computer interpretive report, followed by Compatibility & Conflict for Friendship and Business. In addition to her many years of community service work (including Legal Advocacy and Ethics Development), Dorothy currently serves the community as ISAR Board member, Chair of its Ethics Committee and Ethics Awareness Training.

DOja07@gmail.com   www.planetweather.net   www.facebook.com/PlanetWeatherNews

www.ingramcontent.com/pod-product-compliance
Lightning Source LLC
Chambersburg PA
CBHW032303150426
43195CB00008BA/559